by Jack Thorne

arcola
theatre

First performance at the Arcola Theatre,
on Tuesday 6 February 2007.

Stacy

by Jack Thorne

ROB	**Arthur Darvill**

Directed by	**Hamish Pirie**
Designed by	**Beck Rainford**
Lighting designed by	**David Plater**
Music composed by	**Max and Ben Ringham**
Sound designed by	**Helen Atkinson**

Press and PR	**Stephen Pidcock**
Casting by	**Sophie Hallett**
Graphic design by	**Rory Morrison**
Production Manager	**Helen Atkinson**

With special thanks to Jon and Nora Lee Sedmak

Stacy was previously workshopped in front of an audience
at the Tron Theatre, Glasgow, where it was performed
by Tommy Mullins, directed by Carrie Cracknell,
produced by Hush Productions and resourced
by the National Theatre of Scotland.

Arthur Darvill   Rob

Arthur graduated from RADA in 2006. Since doing so he has worked on *Terre Haute* at the Assembly Rooms Edinburgh and *The Verdict* for RDF Television. Arthur is a founding member of Fuego's Men Theatre Company, performing in numerous roles. He has also performed at the Edinburgh Fringe, Birmingham Rep and in the short film *Intangible*, directed by Nigel Proctor. Directing credits include a street theatre performance in Park Guel, Barcelona. Arthur is currently developing various musical theatre projects.

Jack Thorne   Playwright

Jack Thorne has recently been named a 'Hot Shot of 2006' by Broadcast Magazine following his *Coming Up* drama *The Spastic King,* episodes of *Shameless* and the new E4 series *Skins*. His critically acclaimed play *When You Cure Me* ran at the Bush Theatre, London, in 2005, where he is currently under commission. Jack's other plays include *Paperhouse* (Flight 5065) and *Solids* (Paines Plough/Wild Lunch at the Young Vic) and his short film *A Supermarket Love Song* was shown at Sundance 2006. He is currently writing a film for Celador, an original drama for the BBC's *Decades project*, and a play under attachment at the National Theatre Studio.

Hamish Pirie   Director

Hamish Pirie was Resident Assistant Director at the Donmar Warehouse, 2006 and Resident Director at Paines Plough 2004-05. As director: *PaperHouse* by Jack Thorne and *London Pigeons* by Robin French (Flight 5065, Paines Plough), *Whispers of Britain* (Paines Plough), *Only Hope* (Pleasance Courtyard). As Assistant Director: *Don Juan in Soho, The Cryptogram, Frost/Nixon, A Voyage Round My Father, Phaedra, The Cut* (Donmar), *Epitaph of George Dillon* (Comedy Theatre), *Small Things* by Enda Walsh and *The Straits* by Gregory Burke (Paines Plough).

Beck Rainford   Designer

Beck trained in Theatre, Film and Television at Leeds University. She took time out to study in Helsinki where she began her curiosity for design. After graduating, Beck worked in many disciplines: working on site-specific pieces with Blast Theory and DV8's Wendy Houston, followed by assisting at the National Theatre of Iceland, and designing *Waiting for Godot* for Atlantis Books, Greece. Beck then trained further at the Motley Theatre Design Course, graduating in 2005. Since then, Beck has designed *Hiding* (Watford Palace Theatre, directed by Anthony Biggs), *A Bedroom Farce* (Upstairs at the Gatehouse), *Dogg's Hamlet, Cahoot's Macbeth* (Putney Arts Theatre), *Happy Campers* (Barons Court Theatre), *The House of Bernarda Alba* (Pentameters Theatre). Most recently she has designed for Punchdrunk's production of *Faust* for the National Theatre, directed by Felix Barrett. Recent film work includes *The Other Man* (A Likely Story Ltd, winner of Best British Short Film at the Edinburgh Film Festival), *Lillie* (Cranberry Films) and *Saxon* (Sillwood Films). Beck was recently commissioned by Widen and Kennedy to design a window display, where she designed an interactive horse window stable. Her forthcoming projects include *The Birthday Show* for The People Show, and *A Whale Watching Massacre* for Kisi Films, Iceland.

David Plater   Lighting Designer
Designs include *Company*, *Animal Farm* (Derby Playhouse), *Ballet Black* (Linbury ROH2), *Arab Israeli Cookbook* (Tricycle), *Michael Ball* (Haymarket, West End), *Loyal Women* (Royal Court), *Frame 312*, *Three Days of Rain*, *Morphic Resonance*, *Splash Hatch*, *Summer Begins* and *Badfinger* (Donmar Warehouse), *Dave Strassman Show* (Apollo, West End), *Dark Tales* (Arts, West End), *My Night with Reg*, *Dancing at Lughnasa* (New Vic, Stoke), *When We Are Married*, *A Passionate Woman* (York Theatre Royal), *Moment of Weakness* (Belgrade, Coventry and national tour), *Amy's View* (Yvonne Arnaud Guildford, Windsor Theatre Royal and national tour), *Ballet Black* (Cochrane), *A Thousand Yards*, *The Double Bass*, *Blackbird*, *Mongoose*, *Trip's Cinch*, *Eskimo Sisters* (Southwark Playhouse), *What You Get & What You Expect* (Lyric Hammersmith), *What Now Little Man* (Greenwich Theatre), *Love On The Dole* (Oldham Colliseum and national tour), *References to Salvador Dali* (Arcola), *Oliver!* (NYMT), *Count Ory* (Eastbourne, Brighton, Broomhill), *Girls Were Made To Love & Kiss* (Old Fire Station, Oxford), *The Relationship*, *Falling Through*, *Island Sea* (Riverside Studios) and extensive work for the Royal Academy of Dance and the Greenwich Studio Co. David is Head of Lighting at the Donmar Warehouse Theatre in Covent Garden.

Max and Ben Ringham   Composers
Theatre credits include *The Caretaker* by Harold Pinter (dir. Jamie Lloyd, Sheffield Crucible), *Phaedra* by Frank McGuinness after Racine (dir. Tom Cairns, Donmar Warehouse), *Amato Saltone* by Shunt (dir. David Rosenberg, London Bridge Vaults), *Henry IV Parts I and II* by William Shakespeare (dir. Nicholas Hytner, National Theatre), *What If...* by Layla Rosa (dir. Layla Rosa, London Bridge Vaults), *Tropicana* by Shunt (dir David Rosenberg, London Bridge Vaults), *The Ballad Of Bobby Francois* by Shunt (dir. David Rosenberg, Arch 12a Gales Gardens). Discography: As Superthriller: *Superthriller 1* (Mint Music, 2005), *The Blank Album* (Mint Music, 2006), *Superthriller 2* (Mint Music, forthcoming). Remixes for Beck and Crosbi among others. As Narcosis: *Fright Night* (Industry Records, 2004), *Escape Route* (Industry Records, 2003), *The Bug* (MSB Records, 2004). Remixes for Candi Staton and Kitachi.

Helen Atkinson   Sound Designer
Helen is Deputy Chief LX at the Theatre Royal Stratford East and Head
of Lighting at Regent's Park Open Air Theatre. This is Helen's debut
sound design.

For Arcola Theatre

Artistic Director	Mehmet Ergen
Executive Producer	Leyla Nazli
Executive Director	Ben Todd
Assistant General Manager	Michael John Harris
Associate Producer	Philip Arditti
Associate Director	Serdar Bilis

Arcola Theatre was founded by Mehmet Ergen in September 2000
when he converted a textile factory on the borders of Stoke
Newington/Dalston into one of London's largest and most adaptable
fringe venues. In just six years it has become one of the country's
most renowned fringe theatres with a distinct and powerful identity
both within in the local community and British theatre.

STACY

For Chris Hannan

Characters

ROB, *26, ordinary-looking*

A SLIDE PROJECTOR

ROB *is sitting on a chair, beside him is a slide projection unit.*

Up on the projector as the audience enter is a picture of Stacy, 25 – Stacy is pretty and made-up to look like she doesn't care. She's wearing a funny smile (because she says she doesn't like having her photo taken).

ROB *holds the slide gun in his hand; sometimes he operates the machine and sometimes it's done automatically. Every time a slide changes the machine makes a loud noise.*

A man at the back gives a thumbs-up to show ROB *he can start talking.* ROB *acknowledges the hand and then starts.*

I was at Stacy's street by about 7.15 . . .

He presses the slide gun, it shows a picture of a street.

. . . and the air was the sort of evening mist you sometimes get which you know is bad for you. Anyway, a car came around the corner and I actually pulled out of the headlights of it, so . . . I don't know why. But she lived at Number 33b.

Slide – a numbered tile – '33b'.

The road wasn't one with odds on one side and evens on the other, it went chronologically up one side and then just swapped over the road and carried on counting up over there. Which made it further to walk to Number 33.

Slide – an Olympic walker looking knackered.

ROB *turns and looks at it and laughs.*

I'd bought a bottle of wine too (and I couldn't find an off-licence so I paid pub prices for it, which shows I was desperate to make a good impression, particularly as I knew she had wine in, half of which I'd paid for), so part of me wanted to get her pissed, and . . . seduce her – which wasn't likely by the way – and sort it out that way.

I did have this thing I was planning to say though . . .

Slide – Hugh Grant.

He turns and looks again and laughs.

'I'm the sort of guy who falls in love really easily, honestly I am, I can fall in love in a night, but that's not the same as what I'm feeling now and I honestly didn't realise it till last night. I'd like to just try and behave like more than friends, just to see if it works, because things have changed now, and I know you probably don't fancy me (though she'd been wet during the sex so I obviously was OK) but . . . '

And then I'd just leave it hanging at the end. Like that isn't me not finishing the speech, that is the speech. A cheesy and very very pathetic speech but at least she'll have to respond to it. She won't be interested in a relationship but it's not about that, she'll have to respond to it, basically, and I don't mind being humiliated.

Basically, she could still respond with 'Let's not talk about it now'; that's a worst case scenario. Because I can't say 'I want to talk about it now' without sounding like a dick. Then when I bought it up at some future appropriate date with 'Are you ready to talk about it now?', she'd probably respond with, 'Let's leave it, the past is the past'– she loves phrases like that. Ones you can write on your forehead, do you know what I mean? But that's the worst case scenario.

I stop at gate 17,

Slide – a numbered tile '17'.

because I want to think about my speech, but eventually I get to 33b

Slide – a numbered tile '33b'.

and I stop there as well. She wouldn't be home yet anyway, because she doesn't get home till eight most of the time on weeknights (I'm home at 5.30 – another advantage of my job, and I don't leave the house till 8.30 whereas she's out by eight at the latest). But it probably wouldn't be a great idea to wait outside the house for her to come home, so I ring the bell and hope the landlord or Shona's in,

Slide – Shona's face. She's slightly overweight and she isn't ugly but she isn't confident either so the good bits of her face tend to be pretty well hidden.

as I have no idea what she does and I certainly have no idea what the landlord does so it could be either of them are in. I don't even have an idea why Shona

Slide – Shona.

and Stacy

Slide – Stacy.

are living together, but I think, THINK, this might be Shona's rental.

Slide – Shona.

I think she signed the lease from Mr Martin and Stacy's

Slide – Stacy.

living in it via Shona,

Slide – Shona.

and just took it through *Time Out* or whatever. I bet she's paying 'mate's rates' though – the thing about Stacy

Slide – Stacy.

is she's a brilliant negotiator. Even if Shona

Slide – Shona.

didn't know her before. So I ring on the door but Shona doesn't answer so I just wait in the cold, on their tiny tiny porch, and I have to take my coat off to sit on because I'm not sitting on the ground, not with an arse like mine.

Slide – Charlie Chaplin – in The Kid *– sitting on a kerb-edge.*

They're 33b but actually there's no separate entrance for A or B, in fact there is no A, it's 33 and 33b. B is just the second floor and you have to walk through A's front room to get to the staircase to get up there. Apparently it's illegal for them to be sold like that but it's only renting; the people in A, or the one person in A – Mr Martin – owns B as well. I sit on the step in front of the door, and sort of on top of my coat, it's not exactly comfy but my arse is warm.

I started getting piles aged fourteen and I didn't tell anyone for ages, and tried to deal with it myself, I even went to a chemist to buy some pile cream and the chemist believed it was for my gran. I read books on it secretly, books I took from the library, and I was even embarrassed for taking it then – which is the advantage of the internet now, for kids like that. Anyway I worked out it was sort of a piece that had popped out of my bum and to get it wet and then push it back in. I tried that in a hot bath, it worked, then the pile kept popping up again so I was constantly pushing it back in. Then my pile, when I was trying to shit, exploded, and you have never seen so much blood. I started howling, my mum

Slide – Mum. Unsmiling but pretty. She's fiftyish and she dies her hair dark brown.

came in and tried to calm me down but she was more upset than she needed to be and she rushed me to casualty.

We got done by this really really junior doctor, and I think it would have been much worse for an older person (and Stacy's

Slide – Stacy.

adventures in KY jelly with another doctor were far worse), and he put a lot of padding on it and told me to make an appointment with outpatients (and we did, but this is what my mum's

Slide – Mum.

like: she broke the appointment, cancelled it, when she discovered I wasn't bleeding any more, which I briefly wasn't, but, actually I'm still bleeding till today, so . . . but she said she didn't want to put me through getting the pile sewn up – they put a band around it – and that if it continued I could get it sorted out when I was older), and told me to eat more fibre, fruit and drink more water. But I already did loads of that, I think it was a reaction to my sister, or I do when I'm feeling dramatic . . . Like when I'm trying to do a speech like that . . .

I met a girl at a party and we were hardly talking at all but we got talking – it turns out she started her period really early; aged eight – and she sort of knew but sort of also thought she was bleeding to death (very very heavy flow – always has been – she said it disables her two days of the month, she can hardly move and she has to take them as holiday because her boss – a woman – says that regular illness is the invalid's own responsibility – so she doesn't get holiday – (*Laughs.*) the really weird thing about it was she was trying to chat me up I think). Anyway, it really shows up on the enamel of the toilet bowl – now, when it happens – I sit on a toilet seat and let it bleed because I can't think of anything else to do.

Debbie

Slide – Debbie.

said actually not to . . . no, I'm not going to tell you that yet . . . No. Sorry.

Debbie's

Blank slide.

from work. Another confusion actually . . .

Anyway, I phone my brother again,

Slide – brother. A lot better-looking than ROB*, and he knows it.*

and I never phone my brother, and he's not in so I leave a message asking him to phone me. Then I phone my mum,

Slide – Mum.

and I get through. 'Hello?' – she always sounds as if she's surprised that telephones actually work – I disconnect the call, I breathed into it for a few seconds but I didn't have anything to say and she didn't repeat 'Hello?' again, and she doesn't know how to use 1471.

Anyway.

He turns to look at his mum, he stands up and walks slightly forward to the audience.

It started, with Stacy,

He indicates his mum's picture, he doesn't change the slide.

because she was upset, she'd asked for a hug, then she'd
kissed me, I'd got an erection, she'd noticed – in fact she'd
laughed and told me she noticed – and then it got passionate
quite quickly.

I always actually worry I'm going to smell or something else –
like one of the things girls seem to do more of now, is to put
their hands inside your arse – now (a) I've had a lot of
bleeding trouble with my arse

Slide – arse.

– as has Stacy –

Slide – Stacy.

(b) I can never get it properly clean – it's always sweaty and
sticky, I don't know how other people do it; (c) there doesn't
seem much point – Stacy even tried it (despite her arse
problems) but I moved her hand away – twice – that made me
feel like a girl actually, which was quite funny.

She hadn't shaved herself – I actually think that's more of a
working-class thing (a throwback from the age of pubic lice?)
– and I sort of tried to get that right but I wasn't very good at
it. I was out of practice, and she was tugging at me too but
girls are never in practice at that. Then suddenly she was sort
of guiding me towards her and pushing me in, whilst
underneath me. The (two) girls that have been in charge of me
in the past had always been on top before, and I always felt
blow jobs came first, so this was surprising. Then we finished
and I was on top and asked whether I should roll off now
because they'd always got off first before – and she said yes
and I'd sort of rolled off and then turned on my side to look at
her, because she looked incredible.

But she kept her eyes shut and her tits (the only disappointing
thing about her, they felt too fleshy rather than firm, and felt fat
if you know what I mean, and I'm not a big fan of big tits
anyway) were kind of sagging over and she moved her hand
down her body and began masturbating herself, working

herself up. And I, obviously, had no idea what to do (I struggle with fucking bras after all). After a while I tried to join in but she had too good a rhythm going and her hand was obviously underneath and I never know the exact right place to go neither. So I sort of just put my hand on top of hers and went up and down with her hands, I did none of the work but attempted to feel part of the work. Then I put my face really close to hers so I could feel her breathing, I actually like the smell of bad breath after sex. But she didn't respond to that neither, so I just left her and she orgasmed eventually. On her own. Then she'd rolled over away from me.

Anyway, that wasn't supposed to happen. We've actually been friends since we were kids, and that was last night. So . . .

No. I mean it's not like . . .

I spotted Shona

   Slide – Shona.

quite late, she was struggling with some shopping and it was cold and she was losing circulation on those blue plastic carrier bags that are cheaper than the supermarket ones that cut into your fingers. So I would have helped, but I only heard her when she was about five doors away.

Shona smiles and looks nervous when she sees me, I do the odd gawky thing my dad

   Slide – blank, no face at all.

   ROB *turns to look at it and laughs.*

sometimes does of saying 'Hi' with my shoulders. She smiles again. 'Hi' she says, and I don't reply to that either, I just breathe out through my nose in quite a satisfying way and raise my eyebrows. So we stand opposite each other about six feet apart and she tries to keep smiling.

'Nice day?'

'Yeah,' she says, and she hands me the other bags quite confidently (so I'm not carrying all of them), fiddles her key out of her pocket and undoes the door. 'Come in,' she says. 'Aren't you cold?'

We walk through Mr Martin's front room, which is one of
those scary front rooms that's meant for 'presentation' only,
and the sofa has covers put on them the rest of the time. Beige
plastic covers so as to fit with the room (imagine colour-coding
your sofa covers), and then the rest of it looks so fucking cold:
several crap pictures of birds and a stuffed falcon on a perch
on top of an upright piano, two sofas covered in beige covers
slightly lighter than the colour of the walls. The stairs going up
to B were pine and nice but had a beige central carpet, and just
went straight up, there was no curve at either end, this was a
modern house (and I like a house with an ambitious staircase).

B was all light yellow, I remember how pleased Stacy

Slide – Stacy.

was when it got done and how pissed off that I didn't notice
immediately on entering the house (especially as I'd been told
already about the paint job and enthused about it in the context
of something else). That had been the issue for a while.

'Do you want some tea?' Shona

Slide – Shona.

asks, before we've hardly got up the stairs, she doesn't really
know why I'm here.

'Yeah. Thanks. I'm just waiting for Stacy,

Slide – Stacy.

if that's OK?'

'Yeah. OK.' Shona

Slide – Shona.

was one of those people who are a bit too nice. Like this
morning, when Stacy

Slide – Stacy.

had kicked me out of bed, Shona

Slide – Shona.

woke me – 'Sorry, I didn't know if you wanted waking, Rob.

Slide – of our ROB. *Like Stacy,* ROB *also attempts to convince any photographer that he hates having his photo taken.*

But I figured . . . if you . . . Are you working?' And then she tried to get me breakfast and she wasn't wearing a bra when I was talking to her because she was still in her nightie and she has this weird thing where she tenses her left breast. Not that I can see it now because she's still in her coat and work things.

I walk through the house into Stacy's room.

Slide – Stacy.

I leave Shona

Slide – Shona.

to take the chance to busy herself in the kitchen, and it's a phrase which suits her.

Stacy's room

Slide – Stacy. Then a series of shots which show her room. It's much as he describes it. The wardrobe door is focused upon in these shots.

is pretty bland, she has a bland DVD collection, a bland CD collection. Her clothes are more her, she can be adventurous at times, she doesn't wash them regularly enough but at this moment I don't mind that, I even climb inside the wardrobe, partly because I made a pact with myself not to do anything to upset her intimacy, and I don't think standing in a wardrobe would upset her but it feels intimate to me. I don't stay in there long.

Shona

Slide – Shona.

enters carrying both teas, and she got changed out of her work things into a light-blue top with slight straps (a summer top in November, the first clue of the night).

Slide – the powder-blue top, it's pretty low-cut, some nipples sticking out of it.

ROB *turns round a moment to look at it, then turns back to us with a grin.*

Debbie said . . .

Slide – Debbie, and then the slides reverse back to the powder-blue top.

and some light-blue jeans.

'Are you OK?' she asks.

'Yeah.' She puts down the tea on Stacy's

Slide – Stacy.

chest of drawers and smiles back, then she sits on the bed.

And so I sit beside her.

'So are you two . . . together now, then?' She asks. No, we just had sex.

Slide – hardcore porn shot, the moment of penetration.

And, honestly, the funny thing about having sex

Slide – another hardcore porn shot.

with your best friend is that they are a lot better at sex

Slide – another hardcore porn shot.

than you thought she would be and you're a lot worse.

'I don't know.'

'I thought you were just friends.' She said.

'Yeah, well, we could just be.'

'What does she say?'

'I think she just wants to be friends. Or I know that . . . I'm not even supposed to be here now really.' I laugh, and sort of stand there and Shona

Slide – Shona.

smiles bravely back. They're not really friends, the landlord made it a condition of the lease that neither of the tenants upstairs were friends, Shona's tried a few times (bought Stacy

Slide – Stacy.

gifts, that sort of thing) but Stacy's not that interested, we even talked about it. She thinks Shona's

Slide – Shona.

a bit pathetic, but I quite like her. Though I'm starting to feel really tired, because I was on their sofa all night, and they don't have the heating system on properly in their house and I'm fucking cold.

When I was a kid, and that wasn't that long ago, there was this thing with this dog. He got knocked down by someone in the street and we seemed to live . . . we actually lived in a cul-de-sac. We were the young family in a street of retirement homes and they fucking loved us for that of course. Then this dog got knocked down in the cul-de-sac, none of our dogs, a stray, I think, but I don't know whether those really exist, it was an unknown dog, like a . . . But it wasn't dead, it was whining and thrashing and no one wanted to do anything about it. Apart from my sister, who was always pretty loud, one of these people who made quite a lot of noise. I made quite a lot of noise too, but I was better at it than her. She went out and looked at it, and stood there ages staring and then Mr Parker, who's about eighty, came out and tried to get her away. And then a whole convention of these retired people came out and all stood around Mr Parker trying to get this screaming wriggly girl out of the way, because she didn't fucking care that they were old and didn't really respect the fact that they would break more easily. And so my parents had to come out and the dog was still whining and thrashing. My dad was one of these people that was pretty unspectacular, but still thought he was right about everything. Like, 'Why are we living in a cul-de-sac, Dad?' 'Well, son, because it's a great place to grow up, it's like having fifty grannies,' but it wasn't, it was like living in a place where you didn't bring your friends back because if you did Mr Parker would come over and start talking about the thing you were last talking about with him. Which was cricket or something embarrassing. Though he was great to talk to most of the time . . .

They all loved me, the pensioners, that was a good thing. I'm good with old people, I'm the sort of person who'd probably have fitted in better in the 1940s. I still am. But as a kid it was more like that, I was also beautiful, which was quite important, because old people are letches around beautiful children . . . And my parents loved it, and my sister hated it, she was crap with the old people and my brother just let it ride. Like he let a lot of it ride. My brother was pretty quiet about most of that stuff. But I wasn't going to bring my friends around, because I had them too, and I was quite sensible and knew it wouldn't be good.

Probably I was just better with them because the old people sort of swarmed around me because I was a pretty child, I was a beautiful child. My sister and my brother never were, and I don't know why.

Anyway, my dad made this big deal about saying that he'd deal with the dog. And told everyone they had to get off the road because he was going to have to kill it, and one of the old ladies said, 'No, let's call the RSPCA,' and Mr Parker said he didn't think this was a case for the RSPCA and we had to stand there while they discussed it whether it was a case for the fucking RSPCA and when they finished my dad, who never interrupted anyone, said, 'No, I'll deal with it.' And we all went back inside, but everyone was watching from their respective windows and everyone was trying to work out what they'd do. My dad went and got a brick and then stood there for ages and then he kneeled down beside the dog, and then he got up again and went and got an old tea towel and put that over the dog's head and then kneeled down again and then hit it really hard with the brick. Quite a few times, until it was quiet. And then he came inside and went to the bathroom and threw up and he left the dog out there with the tea towel over its head. So he didn't pull it away. He was quite odd like that, my dad, he had a strange idea what dealing with it meant.

It's funny now.

Anyway, the really funny thing was, the dog wasn't dead, it was just knocked out or something and my dad hadn't done it properly. But no one was going to say anything, my sister tried, but Mum smacked her and said she'd caused enough trouble and she kept quiet. But the dog started howling. Literally 'howwwwwwwwwwwl' – do you know what I mean? It had a broken jaw or something, like my dad had hit it a few times, and had probably broken quite a few things in its head, but he hadn't killed it, and the dog wasn't howling normally, because he had a fucked skull and a fucked jaw and everything, but he was making quite a lot of noise. And we all just left it, even all the old people, because we were frightened of upsetting my dad. Mr Parker was always saying I should respect my dad more and that's what he was doing, respecting him. And my dad didn't go out again because he was frightened and someone else would do it. Anyway, by the next morning the dog had been moved and there wasn't even a stain on the street. I think it was probably Mr Parker, during the night. That's how you behave with dignity, I think.

I know why I thought about that too.

My brother was away actually, on Scout camp but I don't know that would have changed anything.

He turns around to look at the slide projection screen, smiles, and then starts to walk away from it. Then he turns back and looks at us with a smile. He brushes down his lap, even though he's had nothing on it.

'Did you . . .' Shona swallows, then she stops saying anything, torn between her need to keep friends with Stacy

Slide – Stacy.

(which would mean kicking me out) and her need to have me in the house because, and this I know for a fact, she fancies me. Anyway, she just dances around and says, 'Did you . . . '

'Listen, don't worry about it. It's a lot of stuff.' Her left breast tenses again, she sees me look at it and blushes. 'She won't mind too much.'

'But you two . . . last night.'

'Yeah, but we were both drunk, we just need to talk about it.'

'But she doesn't want to talk about it?'

'No. Not really. But I'll talk to her anyway.'

Now, we have talked already, and it was only about six hours ago but as we didn't address it and I have a strategy to get it out of her. Plus, she wouldn't have even had the closure she did have if it wasn't for the fact that I'd turned up at her office, and turning up at her house was actually a better place. What she actually said was – 'You're my best friend, Rob,

Slide – Rob.

my absolute best, I don't have anyone like you, I feel better when you're near me, you're genuinely the most important person in my life' – Stacy is one of these people who's very uncomfortable with sincerity, so overdoes it, because she doesn't actually know what it means. Anyway, we are best friends, we've been friends since we were kids, when my mum

Slide – Mum.

was being shit – and she wasn't that shit, I mean just a bit thoughtless or whatever, I would go to Stacy's.

Slide – Stacy.

She came to mine as often probably. 'You're my best friend too.' I said. I'm not in love with her – I do love her, and there is a difference, though there is also a degree in which she broke my heart. And she thought she'd done it like that, by reminding me I was her best friend and not saying anything else. 'I just ordered your food,' she said, she smiled broadly and craply, placing a ticket with the number basically rubbed off on the table, her thumb was more sweaty than she thought, 'I paid for it, already,' she said, steady as a rock. 'I didn't think you'd want me to stay.' She looked like Mrs Benevolence. 'I want you to stay,' I said, with some delight, as she left me that one open. But she left anyway.

'So do you want it to happen?' Shona says.

Slide – Shona.

Now,

He turns to look at the slide of Shona.

she was really sweet this morning.

I don't know why but the moment felt right to kiss her. So I did, and I never kiss anyone, but I was tired and cold and she'd got dressed up for me, she'd blatantly, blatantly got dressed up for me in her best pale-blue thing and I know and have always known because Stacy

Slide – Stacy.

thought it was really funny that she fancies me. Plus she was sitting beside me on a bed which I'd had sex on less than 24 hours ago, and the sheets blatantly won't have been changed because Stacy left the house before me, and she's a dirty cow. And one thing to be said for sex after a little bit of time is that it doesn't satiate your appetite, it actually reminds you that you have one. She kissed me back, we seemed to kiss for ages, and it was genuinely nice, then she broke off and said, 'But you love Stacy.' With her big shiny soulful eyes. I laugh and kiss her again and she kissed me back. Satisfied I think.

Stacy always used to take me to these parties too, and say things about me I didn't get . . .

Anyway. It wasn't one of those situations where you move quickly. I sort of stroked the outside of her clothes. Shona

Slide – Shona.

was very very feely to the touch too, like her body had been made like that. She wasn't wearing a bra either, and I normally like to touch a bra but if you don't take the T-shirt

Slide – the strappy powder-blue top.

off too soon there's something brilliant and touching a naked soft breast through a T-shirt (I suppose it's an equivalent of masturbating through knickers, also a sort of fetish of mine) and feeling the nipple harden, some girls would have taken the T-shirt off themselves but Shona

Slide – Shona.

wasn't like that, she still wasn't touching me at all. Then she moved her hand up, and I actually was almost still and breathless while she did this, because it is quite sexy, the first time anyone touches you, and she sort of sensed that and almost drew a curve round the top of her head with her hand, still not touching me but watching her hand. Then we stopped kissing and she sort of gently brought the hand down on the side of my head and onto my ear, and she sort of rested in just below my ear, and round onto my neck, and moved towards me to carry on kissing me, with her hand around my neck.

So . . .

I moved my hands down onto her waist and felt the roughness of the jeans, I felt round the jeans onto the thigh, we're sitting on the bed so I couldn't get near the bum but I moved around to feel between her legs but as I was moving my hand towards the between she pulled my hand away with her free hand. So I sort of played thumbs with her hand and then dislocated and moved my hand around her waist again, a waist that did bag slightly over the edge of her jeans but only in a sexy way, and there was that gorgeous gap at the back of the jeans too which girls get when they sit up because they wear their jeans higher than we do, which allowed me to reach down and touch the edge of the back of her knickers and the downy hair that always comes just above that. This was perfect, I felt the sickness of this being very very perfect.

Well, a lot better anyway . . .

I helped her off with her top and she sat there looking soulful so I stopped everything just to look at her and she blushed as I did, but she liked it. Her breasts (and they were breasts rather than tits) were perfect, little pert sacks with puffy nipples that spread over most of them. Most girls lie back for the porn shots because they think breasts look better like that, and they do look aesthetically more beautiful like that, but they look incredible hanging from the front of a body, and Shona didn't have great posture and they sort of hung perfectly, particularly with the nipple spreading over and discolouring them. She helped me off with my top and kissed my shoulder and then my nipple, sort of clumsily, but I liked her being clumsy.

We moved faster now. We sort of pushed back on to the bed, she kept trying to kiss me whenever she could but I started to kiss down her body and then come up again, and I played with her nipple and I even bit it lightly and then I worked down to her baggy belly and then started undoing her flies, while I was down there, looking as I pulled down her jeans to mid-thighs and her knickers just lay there, half rolled down on one side, so I could see the slight beginnings of hair, puffed up in the middle. She was still wearing her shoes and they were slip-ons but she didn't kick them off but neither did she really stop me. I went back up to her face and she was grateful and kept kissing me and I started working my hand up and down her body, and I was fucking good at it, and I was getting lower and lower each time, and I'm sure to look at it my hands looked like windscreen wipers but for once it didn't matter. Then I touched the edge of her knickers, where they'd gathered, and she gasped slightly and I don't make many girls gasp and I stopped to look at her but she didn't say anything (she was looking scared but she didn't say anything, and it was from here that I started to realise she hadn't done this before) and the next time I put my hand down I went over the top of the knickers to just where I could feel the hair starting and again and again till I was down between her legs, and she wasn't resisting me and she let me touch her, and I took her hand down there too and she started masturbating with me, and it was shared masturbation, and she'd definitely done that before and together we took off the knickers. I still had my jeans on though, she was now completely naked and I still had my jeans on.

So I stopped her hand mid-flow and brought it across to touch me through the jeans and she sort of tried to masturbate me through denim (not easy, you get a handful more of denim than dick), and we'd stopped kissing by now, and I smiled at her and then undid my jeans and pulled them down and pulled my boxers down too (the same boxers from the night before) and she sort of took my dick and tried to masturbate me, but she hadn't done it before, and she looked scared and I sort of leaned in my body towards her, spread her legs slightly, and started rubbing myself against the inside of her thigh. She started to protest, and I stopped her, 'I'm not going to do anything, this isn't sex, I'm just rubbing myself, OK? OK?' And I kissed her, I'd literally never felt this in control and we were just looking at each other and I touched her face and she was crying slightly, so I wiped some tears away with the back of my hand, gently, and I moved my hand down her body over her breasts, and down towards my dick which I took in my hand, masturbated slightly, and then put inside her, or forced inside her because she'd never done this before, the hymen was broken (or at least I think it was) but the vagina (or whatever the right fucking word is) wasn't stretched. So it took some pushing. And she made a sort of screech, so I kissed her and carried on kissing her, biting her lips, she was trying to get away from my mouth but she was beneath me on the bed and I sort of pushed her head into the bed with my mouth. I was sort of biting into her mouth in order to keep her quiet, I was almost biting her tongue but it was more her teeth, and that hurt me too. Her hands went everywhere and I grabbed one of them and held it down but the other went everywhere and just . . . went everywhere. She didn't speak throughout the whole thing. I think she would have though, if I'd stopped kissing her.

I think a lot of me is actually down to the fact that I was an incredibly beautiful child. Which I'm not being arrogant about and beautiful sounds like a really funny word, especially coming from me, because I don't sound like the sort of person who says stuff like that. Do I? Anyway, I was the child people would stop in the street to say, 'You are beautiful.' I was actually that child that babysitters would hold on their lap the whole night – boy and girl babysitters. Like, mostly with other children, babysitters watch TV or invite girlfriends over, with me they'd hold me so long we'd be really clammy when my parents got back. Whenever relatives were round, of the three of us – my sister, me and my brother – I was the one who'd get the attention, I'd even get better presents. But the trouble with being beautiful and finding it all a bit effortless is that you get older and it's not so effortless any more.

No. I mean . . .

I actually got in a fight at school, with a guy called Tom – someone – I remember him because he had a weird bulge on his forehead. Seriously, anyway, we fought because he said he was better-looking than me – we were about eight – it was quite important – now I dress like Mr Parker and I'm young but then . . . I was like . . . well, it was important.

I don't know.

She was . . .

When we – when we sort of – finished, and it seemed over pretty quickly, so . . .

She wouldn't stop crying actually. Her lip was bleeding and she was bleeding down there obviously which might mean . . . And she wouldn't stop crying. Not loud tears, just tears. Stacy's

Slide – Stacy.

The slide projector seems to make more noise than it has done previously. Even ROB *is surprised by it.*

duvet cover was a mess but I'd already thought I might clean that. I felt practical, genuinely practical. I cleaned Shona

Slide – Shona.

up using bog roll from the bathroom, I made her sit up, I kissed her on the cheek (she didn't recoil), I led her through into the bathroom, completely naked but she wasn't awake, and noticed her arse for the first time (cellulite) and I gave her a drink of water (emptying out my teacup and using that) and then I put her under the shower. She threw up over herself in the shower so I just left her in there and it was one of those bathrooms with a key in the lock on the inside, so I took that out and brought it round the outside. Then I stripped Stacy's bed,

Slide – Stacy.

and it was getting close to the time when Stacy would be home and I was actually thinking she'd be home early tonight because she was tired, but she wasn't home yet, and I put the bedclothes, Shona's

Slide – Shona.

clothes in the washer –

Slide – Ecover laundry liquid.

mine were fine-ish and I'd do them at home. I actually thought that Shona might explain her clothes and the bedclothes in the washer but might not explain mine. Stacy's

Slide – Stacy.

clothes from last night were still in the dryer so I took them out because I thought that's something Shona

Slide – Shona.

might do.

I went back up to the bathroom and opened it up and she was still in the shower. I went in there quickly with her and washed her thoroughly down below (I remember that) took her out and wrapped her in a towel and sat her on the seat they had in there. Then I went back in the shower, and emptied it of the sick, carrying the sick to the toilet, retching as I did, but the sick had mingled with the blood so I thought that might be bad.

Then I poured Shona another glass of water and crouched down opposite her, my T-shirt was soaking. I felt like a teacher.

'Sorry,' I say. She doesn't say anything, but she's stopped crying, the towel slumps forward to reveal her breasts again. 'I'm really sorry. Um, it's just the Stacy thing, it's made me quite unhappy.' I pull her towel up.

He mimics crouching down as a teacher and then pulling her towel up and then laughs.

Then I get up, wrap myself up (though I leave my wet T-shirt on – because I don't want to take it off in front of her and it seems odd taking it off in another room – and it's fucking cold outside and so it soon feels like ice, the T-shirt, so that's a sacrifice) and check Stacy's

Slide – Stacy.

room for anything and then I leave the house to go back to Croydon. I keep thinking I'll see Stacy on the street, as I walk down her road, and I almost turn off once when I see someone coming towards me, but it isn't her. I keep thinking I'll see her on the tube too, and the T-shirt does start to feel like ice, and maybe it's before, and maybe it's fear but I start shivering. And I'm almost quite pleased I do.

When my sister died – it feels like such a big WHEN, doesn't it? Something Mr Parker would say WHEN the war was on . . .

I was still beautiful then. And I was still the one all the relatives wanted to see, my sister took a while to die, but they came over, to see her on her deathbed, I mean, that dramatic . . . and even then I got the better presents. I'm not joking, though buying a nice present for someone about to die wouldn't be that great. 'You can play with it when you're better.' 'I'm dying.' 'Well, I better give it to your brother then, he's a beautiful boy . . . ' Do you know what I mean?

The thing was, my sister wasn't one of those kids who came into a room and lit it up. She wasn't, because I was, and she was one and a half years younger. I had a little Peter Pan act I did with all my parents' friends, 'You gave me a kiss so I shall give you a button' and my sister would go over to my mum and be stroked while I was performing, but my mum was looking at me while she was stroking. She wasn't completely over-shadowed and I wasn't completely the superstar but there was that sort of dynamic. She was a beautiful child too, she just dealt with it less well than I did, I loved the attention and knew how to deal with it and she hated the fact that I had the attention. When she died I sang at her funeral, and she'd have fucking hated that, I sang 'Empty Chairs, Empty Tables' as a boy soprano, I was quite a late ball-dropper, so still soprano, and still pretty, though that was one of the last times.

Not a dry eye in the house anyway, people still reminded me about that song five years later, still do now, last time was at a dinner party at home over the summer, when we were having another deep conversation about my sister with some strangers. My mum and dad chose the tune (which in retrospect was a fucking funny choice) but I asked to have a tune to sing, so they had to find something and they weren't very cultured, or not as other people might judge it. My brother didn't do anything, the whole service, but he was five years older. He looked after us both sometimes but mostly looked after himself. Mostly we played together and he'd have to babysit every now and again. Though I would say she was closer to him than me.

They rewrote the words actually, and they made me do it over and over and the quite sick thing was, I always thought, for about two or three years afterwards they'd make me do it to relatives or something – I mean I wasn't quite the main attraction at one of their dinner parties but it was sort of 'and now Rob's going to do his song about his dead sister' when relatives (generally old) came over, and they never knew where to look, and it wasn't like they were making me relive it or anything, because they weren't, and I fucking loved performing it and didn't associate it at all (I was young and I had a big ego) but I think it was quite sick now. Anyway,

> ROB *sings his own version of 'Empty Chairs at Empty Tables' from* Les Misérables.

The thing is I'm sure you'll think that it's unbelievable but (a) my parents are quite cheap culturally and didn't realise, genuinely didn't realise and (b) people think they can get away with a lot more with song lyrics, if you listen to them they're all shit – my personal favourite is from the really really lovely bit in *Dirty Dancing* (I'm a whore for cheap romances) and the song goes 'She's like the Wind. Through my TREE.' Do you know what I mean? Patrick Swayze

> *Slide – Patrick Swayze.*

singing a song about having an erection at a beautiful lovey-dovey moment but no one notices because they're watching him drive away in his Chevy and saying will he come back, will he come back, and he does with 'No one puts Baby in the corner.' Nice. Finally (c) I'm probably camping it up way way way too much, to make it unbelievable, but it did happen.

I can't remember much about her now, I used to give her good presents – I remember that because my parents used to give me money to buy them, sometimes giving me more than they gave my brother, with the adage, 'Well, he loves giving presents, doesn't he?' The truth was they thought people loved getting presents from me. My sister knew it every time and every time when it got to her birthday and I gave her her present she'd go over and thank my mum and dad for whatever it was and then come up afterwards and thank me. She was very very clever. That was from the age of about six upwards. I even ruined nursery for her because I used to go from my school to her nursery and stay there after school, because it had a sort of play facility, and what you may not remember of nursery is no one cared what the other kids thought of you, everyone wanted to be loved by the playleaders or teachers or whoever they were, and they loved me.

I used to try and explain this to people, about why I felt guilty about it all, but they'd all think it was me showing off, I could tell that. I never told Stacy about it, I don't think I did anyway. But that's why it's difficult to explain guilty feelings, survivor guilt is bollocks, it's about knowing what you did and why you did it and how you affected that person, and it's not something my brother will ever understand.

No.

I was at East Croydon station by about nine and took the tram up the road. My brother

Slide – brother.

was watching *Spooks* as I came in. And I sat down and watched it too. I thought then I should have taken my clothes off first but I didn't. I was still cold too. It was a repeat on Bravo or Living or one of those things, the one where Lisa Faulkner got her head boiled off in chip fat.

Slide – Lisa Faulkner.

Anyway, the first thing my brother

Slide – brother.

says when I come in (and neither of us say 'hi' when we come in – we never have), 'I had two missed calls from you.'

'Yeah.'

'My phone's off when I'm working, didn't you think that?'

'Yeah. Sorry.'

'No. Just there's no point ringing. I've got a pizza in the cooker, do you want half?'

Slide – pizza. Then another slide, half a pizza.

'Yeah. OK.' I don't know why I wanted to phone him.

Our house is small and scruffy.

Slide – series of shots of the inside of the house, it's much as ROB *describes it.*

We have a porch and most of the time we leave most of our mail in there, or all the junk and most of the envelopes (we've both developed a habit of going to the door in the morning, ripping open anything addressed to us and then leaving the envelopes on the floor; a man from Argos delivering us a new TV told me that he would have thought we'd moved out or were on holiday if I hadn't answered the door quickly). The hallway my dad

Slide – blank.

ROB *turns around again to have another look, and laughs.*

painted yellow and purple, which was pretty outrageous for him. I once worried I was going to turn into my dad, this repressed lump of turd who had nightmares about dead dogs, but I'm not. My room is the first into the house and I look out onto the street, and I sleep on the side furthest from the door (I think everyone does, I haven't met anyone who sleeps closest the door and I've slept with a few people), but that's closest to the street, so when people walk past my house when I'm asleep I could literally reach out and touch them if there wasn't a wall there. Anyway, it's yellow, and busy with posters, it looks like a student thing still.

I found things a lot easier when I was younger, I think. It wasn't that I . . . I didn't get worse-looking or anything like that, I just found things easier. I was a pretty child and popular and everyone told me I was great a lot, so that was good. And it wasn't my sister dying. I didn't mind that so much, well, I minded, but not so it would change my life. I just suited being younger, I was good at it. My brother was crap at being younger, my sister was fucking terrible at it, couldn't get the whine out of her voice. She might have been a good adult. But it was partly that, that made me beautiful, that I was good in comparison and then you get older and you meet people like Stacy and she just is in a different league really.

No. About ten years ago or something I think I could have given Stacy a run for her money. Now? No.

Then there's a staircase (which leads to my brother's room, which is directly above mine, a bathroom and a guest bedroom (we have a guest bedroom, I sleep in it every now and again when my brother's really noisy). Then the living room, which you have to walk through to get to the kitchen. The living room is full of my stuff too, I collect videos and DVDs and I have seven shelves of them. It's yellow too, and has a sofa, which my brother sits on, and an easy chair, which is now really really greasy (the sofa isn't for some reason but you really notice it on the chair), we eat dinner off our laps but there's also a table at the back of the room, and a large phone. The prevailing theme in our house is yellow, like the prevailing scheme (and Stacy's

Slide – Stacy.

house is schemed not themed) of Stacy's, she came round and then copied it, though my dad

Slide – finally we see his dad's face. He looks great, he's a man who's suited his face better the older he's got.

chose the colours, and ours is strong yellow whereas hers is wishy-washy – everyone's got wishy-washy yellow though so although she said she copied it (and I was oddly oddly chuffed about it) she didn't, hers looks like loads of houses, ours looks vivid and dangerous.

'You look tired,' my brother says.

Slide – brother.

'I'm just hungry,' I say.

'Do you want anything with it?' he says. 'It's too late to put chips on, but I could do beans

Slide – a bath of baked beans. A younger ROB *is sitting in it and his brother is pushing it down a hill. They're screaming with delight.*

or something, or toast.'

'I'll be alright.' He touches my shoulder as he walks past and we never touch and he notices how cold I am.

'Shall I put the heating on, you're cold.'

'No, it's OK, I just got a bit wet earlier, my T-shirt's still wet, I'll change in a minute.'

'You should change now.' Me and my brother

Slide – brother.

have this weird competitive thing about who mothers who . . . Not in a . . . Neither of us are good at it.

'Yeah, OK,' and I walk to my room to search for a clean T-shirt (generally I keep my washing down the side of my bed of in a laundry basket) and I'm crying slightly I realise as I peel off my clothes, I peel off to completely naked and I just stand there, and I look down at myself and I'm all red and blotchy. I sit on my bed for a minute, I put on Eva Cassidy on the CD (it's in there already actually – I just press play and I'd have listened to Jay-Z if he was in there – it's just Eva is normally my wank music, if I think my brother can hear me wanking, I put on a CD, generally Eva Cassidy, because it doesn't distract me – it might be because she's dead), and listen to 'Fields of Gold' for a little bit, which doesn't have the most coherent lyric in the world, or at least I don't understand it, and then I get dressed and turn off Eva, and go back out to my brother.

'OK?' he says, and he's putting bread in the toaster. A toaster which burns most things now because the filaments (is that the right term?) are knackered because we've never emptied it (my brother says if we did empty it now it'd properly knacker it so he'd prefer to just leave it and I could buy a new toaster if I wanted one, and I've never brought it up again).

'You sure you don't want a shower?'

'I'll warm up first.'

'That might warm you up.'

'No.'

'You look tired.'

And then I started crying. His back was turned to me and I felt a tear roll out, and then another one, and I tried to walk out of the room but he saw me before I left and followed me. With a sort of 'wha . . . come back, come back. What's the matter?' I mean, both him and me are terrible at this kind of . . . Though I'd be better than he is.

I walked straight up the stairs and locked myself in the bathroom. He was straight behind me but I locked it before he had a chance to stop me. Our bathroom

Slides – a series of slides of the inside of a grotty bachelory bathroom.

is a mess, and it's cold because we leave the window open all the time, and it doesn't smell as a result and it's not horrible, it's a mess in terms of too many toothpastes and too many toothbrushes and old and new razors and a mirror that's never been washed and scuzz in the bath. But it's my brother's

Slide – brother.

job to clean it.

He knocks on the door. 'Let me in, Rob.'

Slide – Rob.

I don't say anything. I actually hold my breath, which is a hard job when you're crying which seems to require more breath for some reason. I don't cry very often though.

'I've just got a headache,' I say, and I did, and had all day, I always get one when I haven't slept or had hardly slept. I can keep going, I have good adrenalin, which is why I think it hits me harder, because my body is either on 'go' or 'stop' whereas most people when they're tired act tired.

'Listen,' he's thinking, you can always tell when he's thinking, 'I'm going to go down and turn out the oven and when I come back up you can be out, or you can be in but I'm going to stay out here, so think about it, OK?' You can tell he's a manager. My parents always say that, they don't get that actually their idea of what a manager is, like a white collar, isn't what he is. I mean, they don't understand that. We're both a disappointment really, but they won't admit that. My dad'd

Slide – Dad.

never fucking admit it, he'd rather take another brick to a dog actually.

Slide – bloodied dog, lying in the middle of a cul-de-sac.

He goes off downstairs and I clean my teeth quickly, I love cleaning my teeth, he always tells me off for flossing in front of the TV, and then I turn on the shower. But I don't get in.

He knocks again. 'I'm back.'

He knocks again. 'I can hear you're not in the shower, OK, mate.'

He bangs on the door. 'I'm worried. Come on. You could be doing anything in there.'

Slide – a dancing girl doing 'anything'.

'Relax,' I shout, I turn off the shower, clean my teeth again and unlock the door as I do, with the toothbrush in my mouth.

He opens it quickly and relaxes. 'What's going on?'

'Nothing.' I wash my face. 'I'm just tired, I didn't get much sleep last night.'

'Yeah,' he puts his hand up so it's on the top of the door and then almost swings on it, 'I was going to ask about that, where did you get to you, dirty stop-out?' He laughs. I wash my face again. 'Shall we talk about it? Did she hit you or bite you

Slide – dog.

or something?' He laughs again.

'I'm fine.'

'No. You're not.'

'I'm fine, alright? I opened the door, I'm not hurting myself.'

'OK.' He sniffs hard then, gets up a lot of phlegm, spits in the sink and then washes it down. 'Will you come downstairs, and I'll finish the pizza

Slide – half a pizza.

and you can eat. You need to eat.' I follow him downstairs and it's not that I don't think about it – what I've done – but I don't think about it as much.

We eat pizza and beans on toast

Slide – boys and the bath of beans.

almost in silence whilst watching an episode of *Will & Grace* (my brother

Slide – brother.

is really really into *Will & Grace*, oddly-oddly over-the-toply into it). But, also oddly, we're sitting by each other on the sofa. He told me to sit on it, when we came downstairs, and so I did and he went into the kitchen to finish dinner, and then he came back out again, put his food down, cleared the side of the sofa beside me and sat down on it. It didn't feel terrible and it wasn't like we'd never done it before, my mum

Slide – Mum.

came up for a week a few months ago (to do shopping she said, but actually she wanted to clean her house) and we'd had to sit by each other a few times then but most of the time our mum sat on the sofa with one of us and the other sat on the greasy chair. But it did feel weird, the sofa wasn't huge so our hips almost touched, do you know what I mean? We don't talk any more after that, but we seem to keep watching the TV for ages.

He was pretty irrelevant when we were younger, my brother was. It's funny, because now he's quite central. I don't know why. He is quite like my dad. When my sister died, they were both the same. Like 'How do we do the right thing, how can we make this better?' whilst hidden behind a sofa. Do you know what I mean? He was a dick.

There's nothing worse than waking up on your brother's lap,

Slide – brother.

particularly as I was pretty sure he had an erection.

Slide – brother, this time naked, in his hands he holds a giant erection.

So I got up as sharply as I could considering I had a broken neck as a result of sleeping with my head at an angle of 66 degrees. I actually never sleep well unless I'm in my own bed on my own, so waking up on my brother's lap on a cheap, small and greasy sofa was pretty unbelievable. Second night on a sofa too, which is odd. I have a mouthful of what has turned from phlegm into what feels like pus. Anyway, I remembered pretty quickly, not that it stopped me (should it have stopped me, I think we're back into whether remorse is a worthwhile emotion, which I'm not sure it is), I eat Weetabix,

Slide – 'WITH-A-BIX'.

I should shower but I don't, and this is two sticky sex sessions later and I leave my brother

Slide – brother, again naked.

asleep. I don't know what woke me up to be honest, maybe it was the erection, I had one too which makes matters worse, I haven't dribbled in his lap anyway.

I eat Weetabix

Slide – 'WITH-A-BIX'.

sitting in the greasy chair and I'm only about three metres from his face as I do and he doesn't wake up so I leave him asleep, Blockbuster can cope. I actually put the Weetabix spoon on to his torso, to see whether he was really asleep, but he doesn't wake up. So I just leave that too.

I half expect Jason

Slide – Jason. Small, ginger, camp, adorable.

to say something as I walk to my desk but he doesn't, he's monitoring a call (probably Shirley's).

Slide – Shirley. Desperate, greasy, mid-thirties and hates being so.

They're all on calls, Tom

Slide – Tom, mid-twenties, cool but not attractive.

looks surprised to see me but winks, Debbie

Slide – Debbie, mid-thirties, suits it better than Shirley.
Attractive in a Meryl Streep-type way.

waves, in a very flirty way, that also was a new thing, she'd
been talking to me all week and sending me stuff, and
yesterday she'd been weird too. Although I left at lunchtime.
And Shirley

Slide – Shirley. The slide-changer start making more noise
again.

looks at Debbie

Slide – Debbie.

as she does and everything seems normal. I plug in my headset
before I turn my computer on, you're supposed to have your
computer up and running but they pay you from the time you
plug your headset in so everyone does that first and then
bullshits any call they get, writing down the caller's BAN
number (sort of a reference number) and the exact details of
their problem which is all stuff we normally do anyway while
the computer loads and then explaining some boring protocol
while you type everything in. Or –

'Vodafone Connect customer services?' And this is the first
time I've spoken and the pus is still there and has mixed with
the Weetabix.

'Do I give you – what is this – a B-A-N?' An old person, my
favourites. Their problems are easy, which is probably a
parable for something far wider. They're brilliant to deal with
in the morning because they don't mind time passing – most of
them are grateful for it. And when the problem is solved they
think you're a genius and sometimes they write in, which means
brownie points, sometimes I even suggest they write in. Tom

Slide – Tom.

hates them, he likes serious problems, Shirley

Slide – Shirley.

and Debbie

Slide – Debbie.

both like men, I like old people.

Slide – hardcore 'grey' porn. An eighty-year-old woman being fucked by a twenty-year-old stud.

We should transfer calls between ourselves, divide the labour.

'That's right, or your mobile phone number.'

'Well, I've got the B-A-N in front of me. Shall I give it you?' He says it like it's a swear word.

'Yes please.'

'492 – '

'Can you give me the number above?' I interrupt.

'Oh. That's right. 1349674313.' I write it down, my computer's not up yet, but do you see what I mean about time passing?

'OK, so that's 1349674313.'

'That's right. Have you got my details now?'

'What can I help you with?' I don't pull it off but he can't question me yet.

'It doesn't seem to be turning on.'

'How long have you had the phone, Mr . . . ' I realise I have no idea what his name is and my computer has stopped turning itself on, so I restart it. I am sweating but it's sort of calm sweat.

'Thompson. Do you not have it on screen?'

'Yes. Sorry. How long have you had it, Mr Thompson?'

'Does it not say so on screen? At least two years.'

'This computer was incorrectly shut down so we're now scanning the C-Drive for errors.' Thank you.

'Right. And what have you tried, to get it turned on, Mr Thompson?'

'Well. Nothing other than pressing the button. It's pay-and-go, I only use it for emergencies.'

'But it's fully charged.'

'Oh yes, I tried charging it.'

'Great. What type of phone is it, Mr Thompson?' The screen finally comes up,

Slide – a computer screen loaded up.

I log in and bash in his BAN.

Debbie.

Slide – Debbie.

ICMs 'I liked your text,'

Slide – 'I liked your text'.

ROB *turns around and looks at it, he's confused.*

she says.

'Oh, I don't know, well, Motorola, it's black.'

I ICM back '?????'

Slide – '?????'

'Can you take the back cover off for me, Mr Thompson?' I wipe my forehead, it's sticky sweat, if you know what I mean, like I've got hair gel in, which I haven't, I just need to wash my hair. But Debbie

Slide – Debbie.

doesn't notice. She looks across at me, she's on a call, she hammers at her keys, she doesn't ever type properly, she hammers, it's like she resents the keyboard for denying her fingernails (she asked Jason

Slide – Jason.

for one of those machines you can dictate to so that she didn't have to type, but he said (a) that would be ridiculously expensive and (b) it wouldn't work in a call centre, it'd try and write down everything – you see what I mean about him? He has thorough thoughts, I always go with the first thought in my head, Jason thinks things through, he's probably the person, at the moment, I most respect in my entire life, and, if I'm honest, he's pretty thick, he's just thorough, which I think is a hugely underrated quality).

'It won't come off, it seems not to come off. I won't break it, will I?'

'No, there should be a button up the top of the back, press that and slide it off.'

'The text you sent me yesterday, you're not going to get me to repeat it.'

> *Slide – 'The text you sent me yesterday, you're not going to get me to repeat it ;-))))'.*

Her ICM slides on to my screen. All the time drawling Essex-girl spiel into her headset, trying to advise some customer that he's been cut off for non-payment. I didn't send her a text yesterday, I phoned though, I think. She's pushing out her tits again. She rubs one of the buttons of her blouse with her platinum ring. Debbie

> *Slide – Debbie.*

didn't know ICMs were viewable by the moderator – like our calls – otherwise she wouldn't have done any of it. But for me, the great advantage of being massively over-qualified for your job is that you can afford to lose it.

'That's right. Right. There's a big battery underneath.'

'Can you take that out?' I dislodge a large piece of pussy Weetabix

> *Slide – 'WITH-A-BIX'.*

which had sort of hidden itself in my wisdom teeth which are sort of coming through and are still very tender, it almost makes me puke anyway.

'How does this come out?'

'Just pull it out, Mr Thompson.'

'How am I supposed to pull it out? I'd rather not break it.'

'It won't break it.' Debbie

Slide – Debbie.

finishes her call and turns to look at me, she sucks in her cheeks and giggles. I don't know what that means. Stacy

Slide – Stacy.

does that too. I presume it's a code, but . . . 'Fine.' He's getting angry now. 'Do I start at the top or the bottom to take it out.'

'Just take it out, Mr Thompson.' I raise my voice slightly.

'No!' He shouts.

Jason

Slide – Jason.

smoothly interrupts the call. 'Mr Thompson? My name's Jason Gould, I'm Rob's

Slide – ROB.

ROB *turns around to look at it. He's entirely confused, he wipes his forehead.*

line manager, if you see the springs are up the top of the phone – it's a Motorola 1133 according to our system – so if you just push towards the springs, push the battery towards the springs then it should just flick out.'

I disconnect from the call. And just sit there. Shirley

Slide – Shirley.

sidles past, she touches my shoulder 'Jenny.

Slide – Jenny, the picture has been taken far too close to her face. She's older than ROB, and not as attractive, but she's smiling. She has 'BLIND DATE' written on her forehead.

was asking after you, you know. Anyone else want a coffee?' she says.

Debbie

Slide – Debbie.

looks across at me – 'Shirley,

Slide – Shirley.

he's not interested in her, she's a dog.'

Slide – dog with his brains bashed out is lying in the middle of the cul-de-sac.

Slide – a number of shots zoom in, like crime-scene photos: an old man is holding a torch and a bloodied brick; he has the brick poised above the dog's head, he's waiting for the dog to show signs of life.

Jason

Slide – Jason.

puts his call on hold, he's angry. 'Can you not talk like that please Debbie.'

Slide – Debbie.

He sounds like John Inman

Slide – John Inman.

Slide – Hugh Grant.

Slide – a pretty little girl sitting in a coffin, playing a game.

with his 'Debbie.'

Slide – Debbie.

'I'm on a call, as is Tom.'

Slide – Tom.

Tom waves his hand as if to say I don't give a fuck. So we all sit there in silence.

'You look rough,' Jason

Slide – Jason.

says softly, when he disconnects from his (my) call. I mean, Debbie is flirting because she's bored probably, but I do feel sick. 'You sure you're OK?'

'Yeah.'

'Switch your computer on before you plug in next time, OK?' he says.

'Yeah.'

'Leave him alone, Jason,' Debbie

Slide – Debbie.

says. They had an affair once, Debbie is happily engaged by the way, but anyway, Jason

Slide – Jason.

had been keener on it than her. She hadn't got to Tom

Slide – Tom.

yet. Or me, properly. 'No, this is my job. Sorry Rob,

Slide – ROB.

there was a memo, switch your computer on first.'

'OK.'

'You had the right instincts about that caller, you just need to take it slower with the older callers.'

'I know.'

'Are you OK, Rob?'

Slide – a child standing on a chair, singing his heart out.

Jason

Slide – Jason.

asks. Debbie

Slide – Debbie.

starts hammering into her computer again.

'Yeah.'

'We need to talk.' Debbie ICMs.

Slide – 'WE need to talk.'

'Come to the cloakroom NOW.'

Slide – 'COME TO THE CLOAKROOM NOW.' Then
another slide with the same lettering on a red backdrop.
Then blue backdrop.

Complete with the campness of the capital letters as well.

He turns to look at it. It changes to a yellow backdrop.

And she looks at me, and picks up her bag and she leaves. Her
shirt is too tight and I'm not sure she's wearing a bra and she
postures away to the cloakroom. One of the functions of the
ICM is that you can forward the same message on and it will
only show its original sender – Debbie – I don't know why it
does that. So I forward it on and I watch, and Jason

Slide – Jason.

looks worried and then goes to the cloakroom and Tom

Slide – Tom.

laughs and does fuck all and this guy from accounts walks past
at great speed and Shirley

Slide – Shirley.

follows him. And I disconnect and leave the office. Tom

Slide – Tom.

watches me go though. Or at least that's how I remember it,
and it feels like I'm remembering it at the time, things are
sliding out all the time.

He gets up, he walks to the front of the stage, then he stops,
scratches his bollocks and laughs.

I catch the tram home and I don't buy a ticket but I'm not
caught. There's still quite a few commuters around but they all
get off at East Croydon station so I'm quite worried I'll be
stopped on the short bit up to Lebanon Road. But I'm not. My
brother's

Slide – brother.

gone by the time I get in so he obviously woke up on time too.

Perhaps he was awake this morning and faked it out, I can't imagine we'd have had much to say. I've got this thing where I pace around the house and I always stick to the same route: up the stairs, along the corridor and back, down the stairs, through the living room, circle the kitchen and I'm sure I look like the Rain Man but it does calm me down. I look on the internet, check my favourite sites. But that's not that good either today.

I try and ring Stacy

Slide – Stacy, but it takes too long coming up.

from the phone in the house rather than my mobile (I don't think she's got my house-phone number stored) but she keeps her mobile switched off at work. She was the one I'd normally talk to, so that was sort of automatic rather than anything else. I try and ring Debbie

Slide – Debbie.

too but she's switched off too, Debbie rings back whenever you call her whether or not you leave a message, she goes through all her missed calls and rings them back, she's very sweet like that, so I don't leave a message, and I'm not going to leave one on Stacy's,

Slide – Stacy.

because I need to get that from new. I wonder whether to ring my brother,

Slide – brother.

but I don't actually have that much to say to him. Then Debbie

Slide – Debbie.

actually does ring, my mobile (when I'd been calling from the house phone) but I disconnect it.

Then the police ring the doorbell (which seems wrong to me, policemen should knock on the door, it's much more action-hero).

And I . . .

You see, my problem is that I've always worried too much about tomorrow – I save up too much and I never spend – I've always not watched a video or something I've just bought or recorded because I want to save it for when I really want to watch it. Then I end up not watching it at all, because I've gone off it. I think I'll really really want to watch it tomorrow, but I end up not wanting to, and I laugh about that sometimes. My brother, if he's got it, wants to watch it straight away. I save money 'for tomorrow', I've got so much money saved and I could do this or that, I could buy a computer, or go travelling, but I keep working at Vodafone and I make a profit off that, taking away my living expenses, I still make about £400 a month on top of everything I have to pay for, because I work shitloads of overtime.

Slide – Stacy, finally it's a different shot, it's her masturbating last night in their temporarily shared bed. We can also see a fretful ROB *peering over her and wondering what to do.*

I'm quite tired and I worry too much about tomorrow, and I think Stacy (he turns to look at her and then turns back to the audience) – well . . .

I'm crying again when I answer the door. I'm trying to smile too though.

Slide – ROB *on the phones at Vodafone. He is laughing at a joke that Tom has told.*

ROB *waits a moment then walks out through the audience. He walks quickly.*

Lifeboat Theatre
in association with
5065 Lift and **Weaver Hughes Ensemble**
present

Fanny and Faggot

by Jack Thorne

finboroughtheatre

First performance at the Finborough Theatre, London,
on Tuesday 30 January 2007.

Fanny and Faggot

by Jack Thorne

Cast   in order of appearance

Part One   **TWO LITTLE BOYS**
1968, Newcastle

ONE / NORMA BELL   **Sophie Fletcher**

TWO / MARY BELL   **Elicia Daly**

Part Two   **SUPERSTAR**
1978, a B&B in Blackpool

LUCY   **Diana May**

TWO / MARY BELL   **Elicia Daly**

STEVE   **Christopher Daley**

RAY   **Simon Darwen**

Directed by   **Stephen Keyworth**
Designed by   **Georgia Lowe**
Lighting designed by   **Tom Richmond**
Sound designed by   **Dominic Thurgood**
Produced by   **Lifeboat Theatre** and
Weaver Hughes Ensemble

There will be no interval.
The performance runs approximately eighty minutes.

Two Little Boys was originally developed and performed in 2004
as *Fanny and Faggot* by 5065 Lift in the Pleasance Courtyard
at the Edinburgh Fringe Festival 2004, performed by Elicia Daly
and Sheena Irving, and directed by Stephen Keyworth.

Christopher Daley Steve
Trained at RADA, graduating in 2006. Theatre includes *The Beard* (Old Red Lion). Theatre while training includes *The Cosmonaut's Last Message To The Woman He Once Loved in the Former Soviet Union, Timon of Athens*, directed by Kathryn Hunter, *Widows, The Broken Heart*, directed by Bill Gaskill, and *The School for Scandal*.

Elicia Daly Two / Mary Bell
Trained at Central School of Speech and Drama. Theatre includes *Fanny and Faggot* (5065 Lift at the Pleasance Courtyard, Edinburgh), *Patricia Quinn Saved My Life* (5065 Lift at the Pleasance Courtyard, Edinburgh), *Where the Devils Dwell*, directed by Rufus Norris (Royal Court), *Eclipsed* (Riverside Studios) and *Dance Hall Days* (Riverside Studios). Film includes *Conspiracy of Silence*, directed by John Deery, and *Dear Prudence*. Radio includes *Riders to the Sea* (Riverside FM and BBC Radio 4).

Simon Darwen Ray
Trained at the Webber Douglas Academy of Dramatic Art where he was awarded the Walter Johnstone Douglas Award for Classical Acting 2006. Theatre includes *The 24 Hour Plays 2006* (Old Vic, London), *The Same... But Different* (Pleasance, Edinburgh), *Nikolina* (Theatre Royal Bath and National Tour), *Romance* (Old Red Lion) and *Capital* (Old Red Lion). Theatre while training includes *Camino Real, Lady Windermere's Fan, Tom Jones, Love's Labour's Lost* and *Victory*.

Sophie Fletcher One / Norma Bell
Trained at Ecole Jacques Lecoq and with the Atlantic Theater Company, New York. Theatre includes *Fish Story* (Pleasance, Edinburgh), *Beautiful Cosmo* (Tron Theatre, Glasgow), *Aruba* (Pleasance, Edinburgh, and Tour including Tron Theatre, Traverse Theatre, Unity Liverpool, Theatre Royal Bath, Birmingham MAC and New York), *Russian Doll* (Seattle Footlights Award Best of the Fringe), *Horror Vacui* (Pleasance, Edinburgh, New York Fringe, and Charleston, South Carolina), *The Ushers* (Pleasance, Edinburgh, and national tour), *Drip* (ICA, London and Theater Zerbrochene Fenster, Berlin). She is a founding member and Co-Artistic Director of People Can Run Theatre Company.

Diana May Lucy
Trained at GSA Conservatoire. Theatre includes *Balm in Gilead* (Mill Studio). Theatre while training includes *The House of Bernarda Alba, The Snow Queen, Nicholas Nickleby, The Seagull, The Beaux Stratagem* and *All's Well That Ends Well*. Television includes *Holby City, Little Britain* and *Bodies II*.

Jack Thorne Playwright
Jack Thorne has recently been named a 'Hot Shot of 2006' by Broadcast Magazine following his *Coming Up* drama *The Spastic King*, episodes of *Shameless* and the new E4 series *Skins*. His critically

acclaimed play *When You Cure Me* ran at the Bush Theatre, London, in 2005, where he is currently under commission. Jack's other plays include *Paperhouse* (Flight 5065) and *Solids* (Paines Plough/Wild Lunch at the Young Vic) and his short film *A Supermarket Love Song* was shown at Sundance 2006. He is currently writing a film for Celador, an original drama for the BBC's *Decades project*, and a play under attachment at the National Theatre Studio.

Stephen Keyworth Director
As Artistic Director of 5065 Lift, in 2005 Stephen filled the London Eye with comedy, theatre and music for Flight 5065, a one-night arts extravaganza. Acts included Damon Albarn, Jo Brand, Boothby Graffoe and the Royal Court Theatre. His own play *Zimbabwe Boy* and three other Flight 5065 shows went on to be performed at the National Theatre. In 2004 he commissioned and directed ten new plays for the 5065 Lift – a 2m-square portable elevator venue based in the Pleasance Courtyard. These included *Honolulu*, *Aliens Are Scary* and *The Powder Jars* by George Gotts. He is a founder member and director of Sleeping Giant Theatre, and his credits with them include *Dog Well Done* (winner of the Amnesty Theatre Award 2002), *The Amazing Adventures of Schroedinger's Cat* and *George Orwell's 1984 School Disco* (both at Soho Theatre). Stephen is one of eight writers on the 2006 BBC Drama Series Writers Academy, and will spend the next twelve months writing for some of the BBC's most popular series such as *Doctors, EastEnders, Holby City* and *Casualty*. His first radio play *My Difficult Second Album* was broadcast on BBC Radio 4 last December. He has written for festivals at the Soho Theatre, Royal Court and Contact Theatre, and he has twice been commissioned by the Royal Exchange Theatre, Manchester. He has been commissioned by BBC TV and Towerhouse Films, and wrote a series of twelve animations, *Monkey and Gorilla*, for FX UK. His first short film *Mother Love* was directed by Comedy Lab director Ian Curtis, and is currently being sent to festivals.

Georgia Lowe Designer
Georgia has an MA in Scenography from Central St Martins College of Art and a BA Hons Drama First Class from the University of Exeter. Her recent design work for theatre includes *Romeo and Juliet, Someone Who'll Watch Over Me, One Flew Over The Cuckoo's Nest* and *A Clockwork Orange* (The Broadway Studio Theatre, Catford) and she has production managed Shapeshifter's *King Arthur* (Arcola Theatre). Her film work includes being Art Director for a short Trop fest film by Elissa Down (Cat & Fiddle Films, Sydney) and Production Co-ordinator for *Future Cinema @ Club Ego*, Edinburgh and Construction Manager for *Future Cinema @ Greenwich Park* (Future Cinema, Berwick Street, London). Georgia has also written and directed a large-scale site-specific performance installation *July 22nd.*

Tom Richmond Lighting Designer
Tom started lighting shows in 1998, and trained at the Bristol Old Vic
Theatre School in 2002. Since graduating with a Dip HE in Technical
Theatre, he has designed and toured with Taurusvoice Theatre
Company, Gonzo Moose, Splats Entertainment, The Caravan Stage
Barge and Bristol Old Vic Youth Theatre. He has also managed a venue
for the Brighton Fringe Festival. He has lit numerous other productions,
and is currently working on *The 39 Steps* (Criterion Theatre).

Dominic Thurgood Sound Designer
Dominic Thurgood is a composer and sound designer, and founder of
the EMD, an acousmatic, systemic and electro music organisation. With
a background in Music, Music Technology and Physics, he holds a first-
class honours degree in Music from the University of York, where he
studied composition under Roger Marsh, Ambrose Field and Bill
Brookes. Dominic works within a variety of fields, having previously
worked as sound designer on *Taking the Blood of Butterflies* (Oval
House, Weaver Hughes Ensemble), as recording engineer for museum
audio-guide *Secrets of the Petrie Collection* and with TIC and Creative
Framework as soundtrack composer for the films *A Fish Full of Euros*
and *Augustus Caesar: Diamond Geezer*. Dominic is currently working
with Jack Sullivan and Andrew Ormerod on *Turnstile*, an audio-visual
DVD, the follow-up to their 2004 project *Camas*, and as a member of
the EMD Collective on their current project, a Siberian electrofunk EP.
www.emdrecords.co.uk

Rebekah Kirk Stage Manager
Rebekah spent two and a half years touring the country with React
Theatre Team and Propaganda? Theatre Company with whom she
acted, wrote, directed, led workshops, and stage managed. She was
Assistant Director and Stage Manager for *Ghosts in the Attic* (Brockley
Jack) and Stage Manager for *Can't Pay? Won't Pay!*, StoneCrabs *New
Directors Programme*, *La Ronde*, Brute Farce's production of *Teechers*
and *The Hound of the Baskervilles* (all at the Brockley Jack). Rebekah
also led workshops with ENO Baylis and was ASM on the final
performances. This year she was ASM for ENO Baylis' *Sing! 2006*
project at the London Coliseum.

Sheena Irving Co-producer
Sheena trained at Drama Studio London and is currently appearing in
The Man of Mode directed by Nicholas Hytner at the National Theatre.
Recent theatre credits include Esther in *Rosalind: A Question of Life*
(Birmingham Repertory Theatre), One/Norma in *Fanny and Faggot*
(Edinburgh Festival), Shelley in *Move*, *The Flats*; *Silence and Violence*
and *Blue Remembered Hills*. Film and TV credits include *Casualty* (BBC)
and *The Hidden City* (Sky TV). Short films include *What's up with
Adam?* and *Miss Heartbreak*.

Timothy Hughes Weaver Hughes Ensemble
Timothy trained as an actor at Manchester Polytechnic School of
Theatre and then went on to study a Master of Arts in Theatre
Direction at Goldsmiths College. As a Producer, recent credits include
Taking the Blood of Butterflies (Oval House), *Valparaiso* by Don DeLillo,
directed by Jack McNamara (Old Red Lion Theatre, Weaver Hughes
Ensemble), *Broken Voices* (Tristan Bates Theatre, New Company),
Wilde Tales (Southwark Playhouse, Key Productions and Weaver
Hughes Ensemble), *Etta Jenks* by Marlene Gomard Mayer, directed by
Ché Walker, with Daniella Nardini and Clarke Peters (Finborough
Theatre, Weaver Hughes Ensemble), *Scotch & Water/Ponies* (Hen &
Chickens, New Company), the Frontline New Plays Season, co-
produced with Rebecca Manson Jones of Spikenard: *Judith Bloom*
(Southwark Playhouse), *Achidi J's Final Hours* by Amy Evans, directed
by Ché Walker (Finborough Theatre) and *The Flats* (Chelsea Theatre)
and *English Journeys* by Steve Waters (Edinburgh Festival, Weaver
Hughes Ensemble).

Julia Stubbs Weaver Hughes Ensemble
Julia trained at Manchester Polytechnic School of Theatre. Her
performances for Weaver Hughes Ensemble have so far included *The
Flats*, *English Journeys*, *The Smashed Blue Hills*, the title role in *Sara*
and *The Silent Time* and she has also co-produced all of the
productions to date. Other theatre work includes the London premiere
of *The Lament for Arthur Cleary* (Brockley Jack), the title roles in
Berenice (Man in the Moon) and *Hedda Gabler* (Etcetera), Nora in
A Doll's House (Etcetera and *Time Out* Critics' Choice transfer to BAC)
and tours of *King Lear* and *The Taming of the Shrew*. At the National
Theatre, she has worked on the platform seasons of NT2000 and NT25
including *Plenty* with Paul Freeman and Stephen Moore, *Long Day's
Journey into Night* with Susannah York and a Masterclass with Fiona
Shaw. She has been involved in a number of readings of new plays,
including the UK premiere of *Desire* by Josep Maria i Benet Jornet
(Royal Exchange Studio), *Waiting for the Z Train* by Sean Tyler
(Salisbury Playhouse Studio), *The Diagnosis* by Steve Waters (National
Theatre) and *Thatcher* by Keiron Butler (Royal Court Young Writers
Group), playing the title role. Directing includes rehearsed readings of
59 Cups by Ali Taylor and *Playing Othello* by Melanie Adams.

Rhiannon Jackson Weaver Hughes Ensemble
Trained as a theatre director at Rose Bruford College where she
directed pieces by Chekhov, Timberlake Wertenbaker and Howard
Brenton, among others. Recently she has worked with Northern
Broadsides on *Man wi Two Gaffers* (Blake Morrison's new adaptation of
Goldoni's *Servant With Two Masters*) and was Assistant Producer for
Weaver Hughes Ensemble on *Taking the Blood of Butterflies* (Oval
House). She is currently developing *Hunger* by Steve Hubbard for a
London production in 2007.

For *Fanny and Faggot*

Stage Manager   Rebekah Kirk
Press Representatives   press@finboroughtheatre.co.uk (020 7244 7439)
        Weaver Hughes Ensemble (press@weaverhughesensemble.co.uk)
Production Photography   Marc Brenner (marcsbrenner@yahoo.co.uk)
Doll Photograph   5065 Lift
Graphic Design   Leopard Print (greg@leopardprintltd.co.uk)

The company would like to thank all at the Finborough Theatre, Robin
Smith and Host Universal, Leopard Print, Mobius PR, Rosie Cobbe at
PFD.

5065 Lift

From 2002–4, the 5065 Lift – a unique 2m-square portable elevator
venue – offered a platform for new talent at festivals in Edinburgh,
Brighton and at the Soho Theatre, London. In 2004 the 5065 Lift sat in
the Pleasance Courtyard and showcased nine plays and fourteen films
from new writers. Commissioned writers include Jack Thorne, Joy
Wilkinson, winner of Verity Bargate Award 2003, Darren Murphy &
George Gotts, both runners up in the Verity Bargate Award 2003, and
artistic director/playwright-in-residence Stephen Keyworth. Comics Mark
Little, Dara O Briain, John Hegley, Adam Hills, Flight of the Conchords,
Will Hodgson and Reginald D Hunter have all performed in the 5065 Lift.
On June 21 2005 Flight 5065 filled all thirty-two capsules of the London
Eye with theatre, comedy and music. Flight 5065 was scheduled two
weeks before G8 Gleneagles, to raise awareness of Fairtrade and
celebrate the transformation of cultural attitudes towards Africa. The
programme included fourteen new plays from the National, Royal Court
and Soho Theatres among others, with music and comedy from Beth
Orton, Damon Albarn, Arthur Smith, Boothby Graffoe, The Book Club
and many, many more. Until 2005 the 5065 Lift project was supported
by Cafedirect, but they are currently looking at different ways of
supporting their work.

Lifeboat Theatre

Lifeboat Theatre were formed by members of the 5065 Lift company as
a way of carrying on the work of 5065 Lift, developing new work that is
adventurous, stimulating, personal, modern, uplifting and entertaining,
and which offers a particular and unique audience experience.

Weaver Hughes Ensemble

Weaver Hughes Ensemble is about the here and now – a new writing
theatre company who nurture new artistic collaborations to develop
and produce new work. Since the company's launch in 1997, WHen.
has produced the work of writers including Sean Burn, Don DeLillo,
Peter Elkins, Amy Evans, Dominic Francis, Patrick Miles, Darren Murphy,
Rhiannon Tise, Paul Tucker, Simon Vinnicombe and Steve Waters.

finboroughtheatre

Artistic Director **Neil McPherson**
Associate Director **Kate Wasserberg**
Associate Designer **Alex Marker**
Pearson Playwrights-in-Residence **James Graham, Al Smith**
Playwrights-in-Residence **David Carter, Laura Wade**
Literary Manager **Alexandra Wood**
General Manager **Emma Reed**
Resident Assistant Director **Alex Summers**
Development Producers **Marie Bobin** and **Susannah Stevens**

Founded in 1980, the multi-award-winning Finborough Theatre presents new writing from the UK and overseas, music theatre and unjustly neglected work from the last 150 years.

In its first decade, artists working at the theatre included Rory Bremner, Clive Barker, Kathy Burke, Nica Burns, Ken Campbell and Clare Dowie (the world premiere of *Adult Child/Dead Child*). From 1991-1994, the theatre was at the forefront of the explosion of new writing with Naomi Wallace's first play *The War Boys*; Rachel Weisz in David Farr's *Neville Southall's Washbag* which later became the award-winning West End play, *Elton John's Glasses*; and three plays by Anthony Neilson – *The Year of the Family; Normal: the Düsseldorf Ripper*; and *Penetrator* which went on to play at the Royal Court. From 1994, the theatre was run by The Steam Industry. Highlights included new plays by Tony Marchant, David Eldridge, Mark Ravenhill and Phil Willmott, new writing development including Mark Ravenhill's *Shopping and F***king* (Royal Court, West End and Broadway) and Naomi Wallace's *Slaughter City* (Royal Shakespeare Company), the UK premiere of David Mamet's *The Woods*, and Anthony Neilson's *The Censor* which transferred to the Royal Court.

Neil McPherson became Artistic Director in 1999. Notable productions since then have included the world premieres of Sarah Phelps' *Modern Dance for Beginners* (subsequently produced at the Soho Theatre), Carolyn Scott-Jeffs' sell-out comedy *Out in the Garden* (which transferred to the Assembly Rooms, Edinburgh); two plays specially commissioned for the Finborough – Laura Wade's adaptation of W.H. Davies' *Young Emma*, and Steve Hennessy's *Lullabies of Broadmoor* on the Finborough Road murder of 1922; the 2005 New British Plays Season featuring Simon Vinnicombe's *Year 10* (which went on to play at BAC's *Time Out* Critics' Choice Season and at the International Theatre Festival, Strasbourg), James Graham's *Albert's Boy* with Victor Spinetti and the specially commissioned *Eden's Empire*, and Joy Wilkinson's *Fair* which transferred to the West End; as well as the London premieres of Sonja Linden's *I Have Before Me a Remarkable Document Given to Me by a Young Lady from Rwanda* and Peter Oswald's *Lucifer*

Saved with Mark Rylance. UK premieres of foreign plays have included Brad Fraser's *Wolfboy*, Lanford Wilson's *Sympathetic Magic*, Larry Kramer's *The Destiny of Me*, Tennessee Williams' *Something Cloudy, Something Clear*, Frank McGuinness' *Gates of Gold* with William Gaunt and the late John Bennett in his last stage role which is just transferring to the West End, *Hortensia and the Museum of Dreams* with Linda Bassett and *Blackwater Angel*, the UK debut of Irish playwright Jim Nolan with Sean Campion. The Finborough's revivals of neglected work include the first London revivals of Rolf Hochhuth's *Soldiers*, and *The Representative*, both parts of Keith Dewhurst's *Lark Rise to Candleford* - performed in promenade and in repertoire, *The Gigli Concert* with Niall Buggy, Catherine Cusack and Paul McGann (which also transferred to the Assembly Rooms, Edinburgh), *The Women's War* – an evening of original suffragette plays, the Victorian comedy *Masks and Faces*, *Etta Jenks* with Clarke Peters and Daniela Nardini, *Loyalties* by John Galsworthy, and an acclaimed series of musical theatre – the**finborough**gaieties – *Celebrating British Music Theatre* with *Florodora* and *Our Miss Gibbs*.

The Finborough Theatre won the Guinness Award for Theatrical Ingenuity in 1996 and 1997; the Pearson Award bursary for writers Chris Lee in 2000, Laura Wade (also for Pearson Award Best Play) in 2005, James Graham in 2006 and Al Smith in 2007; was shortlisted for the Empty Space Peter Brook Award in 2003 and 2004; won the Empty Space Peter Brook Mark Marvin Award in 2004 and was shortlisted in 2006, and the Empty Space Peter Brook Award's prestigious Dan Crawford Pub Theatre Award in 2005.

You can read a full history of the theatre – and of the local area – at **www.finboroughtheatre.co.uk**

friends of the **finborough**theatre

The Finborough Theatre receives no public or private funding from any source, and relies solely on the support of our audiences. Please do consider supporting us by becoming a member of our Friends Scheme. There are four categories of Friends, each offering a wide range of benefits.

Brandon Thomas Friends – Anonymous. Nancy Balaban. Philip Hooker. Barbara Marker. Harry MacAuslan. Anthony Melnikoff. Barbara Naughton. Sylvia Young.

Lionel Monckton Friends – Anonymous. Leopold Liebster.

FANNY AND FAGGOT

For Liz and Jo Thorne

The two parts of
Fanny and Faggot
can be performed together or separately

*Part On*e

TWO LITTLE BOYS

Characters

ONE (NORMA), *thirteen*

TWO (MARY), *eleven*

All other characters are played, as indicated, by the two female actresses. This playing should feel like a game. Indeed, the stage should be set out to reflect this game, with different levels for the actresses to play over.

The audience are seated as part of the action.

TWO *is sitting on the floor as the audience enter, singing to herself, 'Mrs Robinson' by Simon and Garfunkel. She's cutting up a piece of paper to make a butterfly.*

ONE *is watching* TWO *from a vantage point somewhere.*

ONE. Do ya think ya'll finish that today?

TWO. No.

ONE. What'll it be?

TWO. Nowt for you, ninny.

ONE. Yeah?

TWO. Yeah.

Beat. TWO *starts singing 'Mrs Robinson' again.*

ONE. Anything ya'll have me do then?

TWO (*looks up mischievously*). Yeah. Turn round five time, touch the floor n' pull your knickers off.

ONE. I ain't pulling my knickers off.

TWO. OK.

Beat.

ONE. You wanna do something?

TWO. Like wha?

ONE. You decide if ya like . . .

TWO. No, cos if you want me to stop this then it's for something good, innit? You got to tell me something good and I'll stop doing, won't I?

Beat.

ONE. Babysitting?

TWO *says nothing.*

I don't care, mind, if that ain't it for you. You think of
owt . . .

Beat.

Can I borrow ya cards?

TWO. No, they're missing one, ain't they?

ONE. I don't mind.

TWO. You can't play if ya missing any.

ONE. No, cos I'll build something. Can I borrow them?

TWO. If it'll stop the noise.

ONE. I ain't making noise!

TWO. Ya asking me to do stuff, ain't ya?

ONE. Nah, I was saying, but if ya don't want it . . .

TWO. No. I don't.

ONE. Yeah, well, ya being spastic yaself then . . .

Beat.

ONE *picks up the cards and sits in the corner with them.
After some time, she starts to speak.*

JUSTICE CUSACK (*played by* ONE). Mary, I want to ask you
some questions. Have you been taught about God?

TWO (*giggle*). Gad?

ONE. Nah. Don't –

MARY (*played by* TWO *with a giggle, she stands up from her
butterfly*). Yes, sir.

JUSTICE CUSACK *stands up as well. The girls almost
immediately enjoy their game.*

JUSTICE CUSACK. And have you been taught that at school?

MARY. Yes, sir.

JUSTICE CUSACK. Do you go to church at all?

MARY. Sometimes, sir, to the mission.

JUSTICE CUSACK. Sometimes to the mission. Do you know what the Bible is?

MARY. Yes, sir.

JUSTICE CUSACK. And if you take the Bible and promise before God to tell the truth, what do you think that means?

MARY. You must tell the truth, sir.

JUSTICE CUSACK. You must tell the truth. Very well, she may be sworn.

Pause. ONE *leans across and kisses* TWO.

TWO. Why was that for?

ONE. I ain't done nothing wrong, had I? If ya honest . . .

TWO. I was making –

ONE. Weren't for me though . . .

TWO. Yeah. It were. It were a present.

ONE. Nah, ya saying it now . . .

TWO. I wanted to keep it fa surprise. So ya spoiled that one . . .

ONE. Nah, cos you can give it me now.

TWO. Nah. I won't . . .

ONE. Then it weren't for me, were it?

TWO. Yeah, it were . . .

ONE. No.

    Pause.

TWO (*carefully*). I can see a snot in ya nose . . .

ONE. No, you can't . . .

TWO. Comes out a little way when ya shouting, otherlike I wouldn't ha' seen it. I'll pick it if ya like . . .

ONE (*peals of giggles*). I'll pick at it if you eat at it.

TWO *giggles, and pats her friend oddly, and then makes a funny face at an audience member.* ONE *watches her, carefully . . .*

You 'eard about that boy . . .

TWO (*camp, she's enjoying herself*). I AIN'T HEARING about BOYS again . . .

ONE. No . . .

TWO. 'Ain't he got a nice smile', 'He'd look better with his hair slicked', 'Oooh, bet he'd give me a belter', ya like an old bitch . . .

ONE. No, boy that died.

TWO. What of? Knob-rot?

ONE. No. Not that.

Pause. TWO *takes* ONE's *hand.*

TWO. What of?

ONE. Do I talk boys much then?

TWO. No. What of?

ONE. Didn't think I did. Ya reckon we need names?

TWO. WHAT OF?

ONE (*giggles*). I wanna name first.

TWO. WHAT – of?

ONE. Don't know. Workmen found him.

TWO. Where?

ONE. Down Tunstall Road.

TWO. Yeah?

Pause.

ONE (*soft*). What I meant were special, for us, special names –

TWO. If you like –

ONE. You gotta think 'em, mind.

TWO. Ain't you thought 'em?

ONE. No, you're better, ain't ya, at that?

TWO (*giggle*). At what?

ONE. Names, ain't ya?

TWO. How come?

ONE. No. You are.

TWO. How come?

ONE. D'ya wanna play a game?

TWO. No.

ONE. Ya think of them names though?

Beat.

MARY. On Saturday I was in the house, and my mam sent Me to ask Norma if she Would come up the top with me? We went up and we came down at Magrets Road and there were crowds of people beside an old house. I asked what was the matter. there had been a boy who Just lay down and Died.

ONE. Ya think of them names though?

TWO. How d'e die then?

ONE. Don't know. It were probably that 'un workman, with gammy eye.

TWO. Yeah!

ONE. Probably 'aving a creep about, we should play that . . . Do him . . . Do him . . . Go on . . .

TWO starts doing this weird sniffling, and sort of wanders round, sniffling everything. ONE giggles delightedly, then hides behind one of the audience members, and starts using him or her as a shield. TWO *grabs at her, and succeeds in capture, and* ONE *laughs delightedly. Then the girls link arms, kiss and then do-si-do.*

TWO *has a breathless smile on her face.* ONE *picks up her cards and starts worrying the deck.*

TWO. Mam'd do this thing – I wet bed and that, sometimes – and Mam'd stuff my face in it – just to show. But I didn't mind that cos pee ain't bad, good for skin Mam says. (*Giggle.*) No. I minded a bit at that. But – then she'd hang it out back – and make the neighbours stare . . . that I weren't, like – (*Giggle.*) I didn't like that a BIT – AND – AND – ya like this – this'll – yeah – Mam was a prossie an' men that liked me to watch – that was her feature, weren't it? (*Giggle.*) That make ya sorry fa me? Does it?

She taps a man in the audience, on the shoulder. ONE *starts giggling as soon as this starts.*

Can I get on your back? . . . I ain't heavy . . . just piggy style . . . But if you've got a back or anything, like, that ain't bad. But can I? . . . Nah. Lost your chance . . . He smells nice.

ONE. Does he?

TWO. Smell him.

ONE. Nah, don't know where he's been . . .

TWO. Smell him, we'll play smelling, won't we? Smell him . . .

ONE. No.

TWO. You wearing bra?

ONE. No.

TWO. Where d'ya have that off?

ONE. It's mine.

TWO. When d'ya have that?

ONE. Mam said I didn't look right without.

TWO. Can I see?

ONE. No.

TWO. Let us.

ONE. What? No.

TWO. Let us. We're friends, ain't we?

ONE. Yeah.

TWO *touches the top of* ONE*'s blouse.* ONE *flinches away.*

TWO. We're friends, ain't we?

ONE (*hits* TWO*'s hand away when she tries again*). It's not for show.

TWO. If we're friends you let us. Come on.

Long pause. ONE *assesses the situation.*

ONE (*opening up the top of her top*). OK.

TWO (*peering down*). That's nice.

ONE. You think?

TWO. Makes you look smart.

Pause. TWO *stays looking too long.*

ONE (*giggle*). Ya had enough looking now . . .

TWO (*reaching down to grab it, trying to get her hand inside* ONE*'s top*). Can I have it?

ONE (*pushing her away*). No! NO!

TWO. ALRIGHT! Keep ya hair on, ninny.

ONE (*feeling the top of her top tenderly*). You got the neck now. It ain't as good. This top's new an' all, the neck'll go . . .

TWO. You got it yesterday n' all? The top?

ONE. Yeah.

TWO. Yeah? You got lipstick?

ONE. No.

TWO. Me mam brought lipstick, so . . .

ONE. Nah, you nicked it . . .

TWO. Nah, she gave us . . .

ONE. No . . .

TWO. She gave it us, OK? (*Giggle.*) Ninny.

MR LYONS (*played by* ONE). You said that while Norma was killing Brian she made a screaming noise.

MARY. She did.

MR LYONS. Did you think she was mad?

MARY. I just thought she had gone out of her mind.

MR LYONS. You told the court that you said to Norma, after Brian was dead, 'I should tell the police, but I'm not going to.' Is that right?

MARY. Yes.

MR LYONS. Why did you say that to Norma?

MARY. Because I was not going to tell the police and Norma thought I was. 'Oh, if I told the police that May done it,' she said – to herself – 'I will be on the better side of the police' – that is what she thought.

MR LYONS. I don't understand. Will you say that again?

MARY. I was not going to tell the police but Norma says, 'Oh,' she says, she thinks to herself, 'Oh, if I tell the police, I will be on the better side of them and May will get all the backwash' – that is what she thought.

Beat.

ONE. What do you wanna do then?

TWO. Be sisters. You want that?

ONE (*crooked smile*). We can't be sisters.

TWO. Yeah. There's a way.

ONE. Yeah?

TWO (*giggle*). Then your mam'll buy clothes for me an' all.

ONE. No.

TWO. And a bra.

ONE. When ya need it.

TWO. You don't reckon straightaway?

ONE. No, cos Lizzie ain't got one.

TWO. That case, not then.

ONE. Not what?

TWO (*giggle*). Knob-rot?

> *Beat.* ONE *smiles, confused.*

ONE. What do we do though? For sisters –

TWO. Share blood, donut. Cut wrists and share blood.

ONE. I don't like that.

TWO. You have ta.

ONE. Don't want your mam neither.

TWO (*giggle*). It's alright, we'll live with yours, n' come to mine for special, you got thing to cut with?

ONE. No. Do you mind?

TWO. What?

ONE. I don't like blood, so . . .

> *Pause.*

MR LYONS (*played by* ONE). But you mentioned 'throat'. You didn't say, did you, that Norma had hit him on the head and killed him?

MARY. No.

MR LYONS. Why did you decide to talk about throat?

MARY. Well, you see . . . you see that on television, on the *Apache* and all that.

MR LYONS. Didn't you also see on television people being killed by being hit on the head with something?

MARY. It does not kill them, it just knocks them out.

MR LYONS. Which one of you was supposed to be 'Fanny' and which of you was supposed to be 'Faggot'?

MARY. I was supposed be 'Faggot'.

MR LYONS. Just look at Note 4, Exhibit 15. Just look at the front of it. Is that your writing?

ONE pulls off a sheet or raises a blind to reveal a note on the wall, written in lipstick:

> *You are micey*
> *y Becurse*
> *we murdered*
> *Martain Go*
> *Brown you Bete*
> *Look out THERE*
> *are Murders about*
> *By FANNYAND*
> *and auld Faggot*
> *you Srcews.*

TWO. My mam . . . (*She reconsiders the sentence.*)

Beat.

MARY. I think so.

MR LYONS. Yes. Now, does it say, 'You are micey'? Does 'micey' mean stupid?

MARY. Yes.

The girls giggle at each other, then TWO turns around portentously and leads on with the prosecution.

MR LYONS (*now played by TWO*). And who is the 'you'? Does it mean the police?

Pause.

MR LYONS (ONE *takes over the part*). Did you mean the police were stupid?

MARY. I don't know. We just put it down. Everyone.

MR LYONS. Yes, you were showing the police how clever you were, weren't you?

MARY. How?

MR LYONS. What?

MARY. How?

MR LYONS. Well, you knew that you knew something about Martin Brown's death that the police didn't know?

MARY. He was before.

NORMA (*played by* ONE). Yeah.

MARY. Martin Brown –

NORMA. Martin George Brown.

MARY. An' then Brian.

NORMA. Yeah.

MARY. I never knew nothing about it. The police knew more 'n me.

TWO *sits down, she looks about, kneels up, scratches herself and sits down again. She picks up her butterfly and unfolds it.*

ONE (*giggle*). Shall we marry? Don't wanna be sisters or that, but we could have a marrying –

TWO. Go 'ave honeymoon at corpse spot.

ONE. Yeah. If ya like.

TWO. No. Sisters or nothing, I reckon I could get nails pretty sharp. I could cut you with me nails.

ONE. No.

TWO. I could saw ya with me nails. If I pinched, it would bleed. I could do you with these even – (*She gestures to the scissors.*)

ONE. No.

TWO. Sisters or nothing.

ONE. Nothing then.

Pause. TWO *appraises the situation with distaste.*

TWO. You got crap skin anyway, take a proper saw to get through that.

ONE. No, you got crap skin.

TWO. You got scabs we could have a pick at?

ONE. We could shake. Spit on it and shake out.

TWO. I ain't touching ya spit!

ONE. Well, that's final offer, ain't it?

TWO. Ooooooh. What turned you into madam?

ONE. NO!

TWO (*giggle*). Don't ya wanna be my sister, ninny?

ONE. No, I don't like blood, that's that –

TWO. Ninny goat.

ONE. No, I ain't, promise.

TWO. Ninny.

ONE. NO! I DON'T WANT. YOU JUST WANT – me mam.

Beat.

TWO (*quiet*). No.

TWO *hunches her shoulders.*

ONE *realises her mistake and tries to resurrect herself.*

Pause.

ONE. Ya my best friend though.

TWO *doesn't reply.*

ONE *leans across and kisses her.* TWO *wipes the kiss off her face.*

ONE. You are. Let's get married n' that.

> *Beat.* TWO *shoots a sly smile away from* ONE. ONE *cranes her head to look.*

I'll do anything else, to show.

TWO *doesn't reply.* ONE *strokes her.*

ONE. Don't you want to play or owt?

> *Pause.* ONE *strokes her face.*

We could go to that man's again, ya mam's friend . . . He's nice . . . gives us stuff . . . Come on.

> ONE *holds* TWO*'s cheeks and attempts to prise her tongue out of her mouth. Pushing her cheeks hard to attempt to get her teeth open so she can get at her tongue. She fails. She slaps* TWO.

Come on. Come on, dummy. We could go see corpse even . . . go see boy . . .

> *Beat.*

TWO. OK.

ONE. Could we?

TWO (*low*). You wanna see corpse?

ONE. Mibbe.

TWO. You reckon we can . . .

> ONE *kisses* TWO.

ONE. I don't want ya mam. Sorry. That's all.

TWO. Is there blood?

ONE. What?

TWO. Did gammy eye kill him with blood?

ONE. I don't know.

TWO. Think though, what do you reckon?

ONE (*giggle*). Yeah, smacked him with a spade, innit?

TWO. Yeah?

ONE. No, don't want to see corpse.

TWO. No, cos you promised.

ONE. No, I never. You just don't want to go on ya own, innit?

TWO. No.

ONE. Yeah.

TWO. No.

ONE. I don't want to see him dead.

TWO (*mimicking*). 'I don't want to see him dead.' Dreary head. Spastic.

ONE. I ain't bein' soft, I just don't wanna see him dead. Could break in school if you like, I'll do that.

Pause.

ONE. Could get married though – like I say –

TWO. I wanna be SISTERS not MARRIED . . .

ONE. Truth or dare, we could, if you wanna?

TWO. Truth. What's worst you done, with boys?

ONE (*no hesitation*). Belly job. What's worse you done?

TWO. Nah, I don't care. Dare. Go bring corpse back.

ONE. No! I don't want that.

> *Pause.*

Truth. Which boys ya like?

TWO. WHAT? How does that work? Ya can't have that.

ONE. Danny, innit?

TWO. You say no dare then I got to say truth . . . Ain't fair.

ONE. No, cos you got a truth.

TWO. No, I said dare . . .

ONE. You said truth first.

TWO. I can change mind.

ONE. Yeah, OK. You can give us another dare then . . . but I ain't doin' that . . .

TWO. Take off ya top, I want to see bra again.

ONE. No, I ain't doing . . . no . . .

TWO. What's point in dares then?

ONE. No. Say another.

TWO. Let me make you me sister.

ONE. NO!

TWO. Take off ya top then. You can't have three no dares.

ONE. I don't want to.

TWO. You let him see it. No one's looking anyway, they ain't that great . . .

ONE. Well, he's different, int he?

TWO (*starts to wrestle with the bottom of* ONE*'s top*). I'll give you sweets if you like, I'll get'm from shop. What sweets he get ya?

ONE. Nah, he never, I don't want to.

TWO. I'm nice, ain't I?

ONE. No.

TWO. How come ya my friend then?

ONE. What?

TWO. Go get corpse or do sisters or get ya top off. Go on.

TWO *stops wrestling. Pause.*

Piss off then.

ONE. It's my street an' all.

TWO. No.

TWO *walks up to the piggyback man she talked to before. She attempts to get on his back.* ONE *giggles, she is less good at sulking than* TWO.

See?

Pause.

MR LYONS (*played by* TWO). I want you to look at Note 1, please, Exhibit 12.

She bangs the side of the stage hard, it makes a great big noise, so she bangs it again.

You wrote that, is that correct?

JUSTICE CUSACK (*played by* TWO). Yes, she said that.

MARY. Cos he was always joining in for her, the Judge, and she was thirteen, so that ain't right. He didn't want her booing in the court and that, but he didn't join in.

NORMA. I said I wrote all of it; I don't know . . .

MR LYONS. Look at Note Number 2, please, Exhibit 13. Can you see the words in the middle, 'we murder'?

TWO *snatches the lipstick up and writes quickly on the wall:*

> *fuck of*
> *we murder*
> *watch out*
> *Fanny*
> *And Faggot*

NORMA. Not by me.

MR LYONS. Now just think. Isn't that your writing, Norma?

NORMA. No.

MR LYONS. Look at Note Number 1, Exhibit 12.

NORMA. I don't want to.

MR LYONS. Can you see the word 'murder' there?

NORMA. No.

Beat. NORMA *folds into herself.*

No.

Pause. NORMA *snivels effectively.*

JUSTICE CUSACK (*played by* TWO). Well, Mr Lyons, this gets increasingly difficult and I appreciate your difficulties, but it is obvious that this child shows great reluctance to deal with these notes at all and really doesn't want to look at them. You must pursue the matter if you think right, but detailed examination, at any rate, may not achieve any purpose. You see, Mr Lyons, you have your duty to discharge on behalf of the Crown. I, on the other hand, not only have to conduct the trial but to see that, in the case of a young child, not too much distress is caused.

MARY. He said that. That's when it started . . .

TWO. Let's go find that boy . . .

ONE. Dead one?

TWO. Yeah?

ONE. No. NO. I don't want that. I said that.

TWO. Take off ya top then! I'm going back to makin' butterfly otherlike, cos this is boring.

ONE. You got to an' all then. Take off ya top an' all . . .

TWO. I'm a little girl though . . .

ONE (*turning to audience*). No. I get it. No.

TWO. Younger, ain't I?

ONE. Nah, cos if you want to, you got to show too.

TWO. I ain't got bra on.

ONE. But if you want mine, you got to take your top off an' all then.

TWO. I ain't got a bra on.

ONE. Then I ain't . . .

   Pause.

TWO. OK.

   Beat. They size each other up – did TWO *really just say 'OK'. Yes, she did.*

ONE (*giggle*). You first.

TWO. No.

ONE. You go first an' I'll take my top off an' all.

TWO. No.

ONE. Together then.

TWO. OK.

ONE. I'll count three.

TWO. OK.

ONE. Just a sec though . . . You stand there. I'll stand 'ere an' you gotta stand, like, there.

TWO. OK.

ONE. One . . . Two . . . Three.

Neither of them moves.

ONE. You had ya chance then.

TWO. You sound like Mam.

ONE. Nah, I don't, cos I ain't.

TWO *takes her top off, she is naked underneath.*

TWO. Your turn.

ONE. OK.

ONE *takes her top off and she is wearing a bra.*

TWO. You look smart.

ONE. Thanks . . . you look nice an' all.

TWO. You like 'em, do you?

ONE (*little giggle*). What?

TWO. My tits.

ONE. They're OK . . . you like my mine?

TWO. Can't see. A big bra in the way.

They both giggle.

ONE. I ain't taking bra off.

TWO. You've seen mine though, ain't ya?

ONE. Mine are bigger 'n yours.

TWO. Well, that ain't a nice thing to say.

Pause.

TWO. Take it off and then we'll get dressed.

Pause.

ONE. We'll get trouble if any of 'm sees it like this.

TWO. I don't care.

ONE. No. Me neither.

TWO. Take off bra then.

ONE. Nah. An' I ain't gonna so you can quit that –

TWO. Go on.

ONE. No.

TWO. Donut.

Pause.

ONE. You wanna get dressed then?

TWO. If ya like.

ONE *puts her top on.* TWO *just stands there.*

ONE. You ain't getting dressed?

TWO. No.

ONE. How come?

TWO. Yours are bigger 'n mine.

ONE. Nah. Doesn't mean you shouldn't get dressed, does it?

TWO. No? You don't reckon?

Pause.

MAN (*played by* ONE, *putting on a deep voice*). Come over here.

They both giggle.

TWO (*trying to imitate* ONE*'s voice*). Come over here.

They giggle again, and then they look at each other and come over all serious.

MAN. Come over here.

TWO. No.

MAN. Don't you want to come over here?

TWO. No.

MAN. Come over here. I won't hurt you.

MARY. I don't want to go over there.

MAN. Come on, darling, I'm not going to hurt you.

MARY. I know.

MAN. So come on.

MARY. I don't want to.

MAN. Even for me? Even for your mum?

MARY. No, what's she said? No.

MAN. Do you mind if I go over to you?

MARY. Yes.

MAN. Free country, isn't it? I am going to come over to you, May.

MARY. Mam?

MAN. I think you're a really pretty girl.

MARY. Mam!

MAN. You have a lot to be proud of, young lady.

MARY. Mam! Mam! (*Long hard scream.*) MAM!

Beat. MARY *looks around wildly.*

Beat. MARY *forces herself out of the picture. Tears* TWO *back out again.*

TWO. I'm prettier though, ain't I?

ONE. Than what?

TWO. You. I'm prettier than you.

ONE. Who says.

TWO. My mam's prettier 'n yours. Makes sense.

ONE. Yeah, but she ain't right, is she?

Pause.

How come it's always true with you? How come you always say it like it's true?

Beat.

TWO. I don't.

ONE. You do.

TWO. No. I know. See?

ONE. What?

TWO (*giggle*). I never said that like it's true, did I?

ONE. What?

TWO. Why do you cry all the time? Eh? Cos that ain't right?

TWO *starts walking around the theatre, trying to touch the side all the way around, disturbing the audience massively as she does. She walks quickly.*

(*Advancing dangerously towards* ONE.) Where do you think we shoulda gone? If we'd run?

ONE. South. Where do you . . .

TWO. North, stick out less.

ONE. South.

TWO. Don't be a cockhead, we'd have gone north.

ONE (*big giggle*). NO! SOUTH! COCKHEAD!

ONE *slips behind one of the audience members and just stands there giggling, suddenly manically full of energy.* TWO *attempts to touch her, but* ONE *dodges this way and that, hiding behind different audience members as she does so.* TWO *starts enjoying it, dodging all the time. The girls giggle as they play. When they stop playing, they're both breathless.* ONE *gets out the packet of cards again and begins to count them. She leaves some on the floor, the rest she puts back in her pocket.*

TWO. I wanna go see that body . . .

ONE. I do. Too. Sometimes . . . but after a think I don't.

TWO. I won't let you wet your pants or nothing, I'll be nice and that . . .

ONE. No . . . sorry.

TWO. Come on . . .

ONE. Why won't you go on your own?

TWO. Cos it'll be better with you, then we can talk n' that . . .

ONE. Are you scared? Cos that'd make it better . . .

TWO. Yeah. But think of it . . .

ONE. No.

Pause. TWO *stares contemptuously at* ONE.

TWO. I ain't scared really.

ONE *approaches* TWO *cautiously, then touches her, and then pulls her close and whispers in her ear, then* TWO *starts behaving like a small child.*

ONE (*to victim*). It's OK, pet –

TWO. Where's Gamma?

ONE. Lie down. You wanna blanket? It's clean, mind, the floor . . .

TWO. Where's Gamma?

Beat. ONE *can't stop herself from getting a fit of the giggles.*

ONE. Where's Gamma?

TWO. WHERE'S GAMMA?

ONE. I'll do it.

She carefully helps TWO *onto the floor, and lays out her left hand away from the body.*

TWO. No. Like this . . .

They swap over, now ONE *is being moulded into a corpse shape by* TWO. TWO *opens* ONE'*s mouth and then giggles and puts her finger inside.* ONE *splutters it out and* TWO *giggles. Then* TWO *pulls* ONE'*s top up and draws a butterfly on her belly.*

ONE. But that were blood . . .

TWO. And there was stabs like – and they'd pulled his pants down and had a fiddle and they'd cut this – (*She gestures to her inner thigh.*) open . . .

TWO *starts to giggle.* ONE *can't resist and joins in, they keep giggling for ages.*

MARY. But they believed her cos she acted like a spastic in court.

MR SMITH (*played by* TWO). Where did you go to?

NORMA. Up our back lane.

MR SMITH. Up your back lane. What did you do?

Beat.

(*Prompting.*) You went up your back lane.

NORMA. Of Linda Routledge.

MR SMITH. What did you do?

NORMA. For about twenty minutes we were making pom-poms.

During the following, ONE *finds her half-made pom-pom and continues to wind it.*

JUSTICE CUSACK (*played by* TWO). Don't lump the two girls together in respect of any particular count. It is quite open to you to find different verdicts with regard to each of the two girls, if you think that is right. But your approach must not be, and I am sure it will not be, to say either on the one hand, without really considering the evidence, 'Poor little girls, we will let them go,' or, on the other hand, 'Nasty little girls, we will convict them.' Your task, I'm afraid, is much more detailed than that: you must consider separately what is proved with regard to each girl, and with regard to each charge in the indictment. They are charged, as you know only too well, with Murder, indeed with two Murders, and the prosecution say that each girl is guilty of those Murders. The situation is this: if any unlawful killing occurs and two people participate in it, it does not matter whose hand actually does the deed. If one person commits the act which causes the death, and the other is present and knows what is intended and what is happening and is either helping or ready to help, that person is equally guilty. Help may be given, not only actively, but by keeping a look-out; heading other people off or helping to attract or to detain the victim. If however, the person is there as a mere spectator and not there to help and not giving any help, that person cannot be held responsible. It may be wrong that a person should remain as a spectator to something that is to most people obviously repugnant, but it is not a criminal offence until they are participating in what is going on in some degree.

TWO *stops and watches* ONE *making her pom-pom. She watches for as long as a minute.*

TWO (*to audience, soft as anything*). What does immature mean? Serious, like, what? (*She waits for a response.*) Cos she was there n' all, so does. Cos is she and me not? How come I ain't then? ... Does that mean I get blame? ... How come she's older then?

TWO *hits the side of the stage, then hits it again, then hits it hard continually. Beating out a painful rhythm, then she turns back and smiles duplicitously.*

An' I got excuse. Though weren't proper to tell 'em about my mum. She'd a said it weren't like that anyway. An' Norma's mum were better at smiling – an' she smiled a lot – Norma were always turning round and smiling and she was telling her to face front, but my mum told me to just sit there, so I did, stone cold, an' they thought that made me worse.

TWO *takes* NORMA's *hand. Their joined hands swing.* NORMA *giggles.*

MARY. It were your fault though.

NORMA. No.

MARY. It were.

NORMA. No.

MARY. It were your fault though . . .

NORMA. No.

MARY. It were YOUR FAULT!

NORMA. No! YOURS!

MARY. NO! YOURS! YOURS! YOURS! (*She starts hammering on the walls.*) YOURS! YOURS! YOURS!

NORMA *puts her fingers in her ears and screams as loudly as she can. A lingering pause.*

ONE. You wanna play a game?

TWO. No.

ONE. You wanna play spitting?

TWO. No.

ONE. I'll go see body if ya like . . .

TWO. No, don't want that now . . .

ONE. I'll go with ya . . . If ya nice, if we're friends again . . .

TWO. I DON'T WANT that. Not now . . . OK?

ONE. Ya don't wanna be friends?

TWO. I don't want nothing. Not at the minute.

Pause.

ONE. You don't think we're friends no more?

TWO. Not at the minute.

ONE (*tries to pull* TWO, *but she stays stock-still*). Come on,
  let's go to the body, I'll do it now. I'll do sisters n' all . . .

TWO. No. Not at the minute. I'm thinkin', ain't I?

ONE. No. Come on. If we're friends n' that . . .

TWO. NO!

ONE. You scared?

TWO. No.

ONE (*giving up on pulling and hugging* TWO). Come on.
  That's better. We're friends n' all now. Let's go.

TWO. No.

  ONE *hugs her again, but this time* TWO *prevents her, so
  she only ends up hugging half of* TWO.

ONE. Come on.

TWO. No.

ONE (*now pulling* TWO). Come on.

TWO. No.

ONE (*screaming*). COME ON.

  Pause. ONE *goes limp.*

TWO. No. We both done it, but we're too young –

ONE. No.

TWO. You lied n' all. Blaming me. An' ya mam's good.

ONE. Mam's ain't to do with it . . . Ain't an excuse for nowt.

TWO. No. Ya remember how ya mam'd sing with us? 'Mrs
  Robinson' n' that, when she's putting out the washing . . .

ONE. She never liked you. Didn't trust ya round me, said it were your eyes, or your mam . . .

TWO. She liked me some though . . .

NORMA. No.

JUSTICE CUSACK (*quicker now, played by* ONE). Do you go to church at all?

MARY. Sometimes, sir, to the mission.

JUSTICE CUSACK. Sometimes to the mission. Do you know what the Bible is?

MARY. Yes, sir.

JUSTICE CUSACK. And if you take the Bible and promise before God to tell the truth, what do you think that means?

MARY. You must tell the truth, sir.

TWO. An' that was right, cos I never thought it was forever. So . . .

ONE. No, but if ya brother died you'd know . . .

TWO. I ain't got a brother.

ONE. Yeah.

TWO. No.

ONE. Ya have though. To imagine him . . .

TWO. Can't . . .

ONE. If one of mine though, you'd know it? If he died?

TWO. She's got ten, and one of them's spastic. They liked her for that n' all . . .

ONE. Nah, you'd know though, someone goes 'Norma's brother's dead', you'd say. 'That's forever.'

TWO. Which one?

ONE. No. May . . .

TWO. Yeah, but if it ain't like that then it ain't forever . . . Which brother?

ONE *pushes* TWO *hard down onto the floor, and pulls her hair.* TWO *doesn't respond.*

ONE. No!

MR SMITH (*played by* ONE). It is not part of my duty to blackguard Mary or blacken her character. Although this is a ghastly case, and although some of the evidence may have made you ill, it is possible to feel sorry for Mary.

MARY. An' you n' all.

MR SMITH. She had a bad start in life. Her illness – psychopathic personality –

MARY. But how come you ain't got that?

MR SMITH. – is said to be the result of genetic and environmental factors. It's not her fault she grew up this way; it's not her fault she was born.

MARY. He said that . . .

Long pause. MARY *picks up the playing cards that* ONE *left on the floor. She picks as* NORMA *speaks.*

ONE. Can we not want to do something then?

TWO. I'M HAVIN' A MINUTE . . .

ONE *giggles, then lets her smile fade.*

ONE. Shall we go see body? Come on, sleepy-head.

TWO. Ain't we done this?

ONE. So what you wanna to do then?

TWO. Nowt, I got a headache, ain't I?

ONE. You wanna get married. (*Sings.*) 'Here comes the bride, big, fat and wide. They couldn't get her into the church. So she had to be married outside.'

She bends and whispers something in TWO's *ear. She expects a laugh, she doesn't get one.*

I, uh – (*Soft.*) I'll be sisters if ya like . . .

TWO. I wanna be lonely for a bit though.

ONE. Do gammy-eyed man again.

TWO. Piss off. Go look for boys.

ONE. I don't like 'em though. I don't. I don't like boys.

TWO. Piss off.

ONE. Come on . . . sisters, you can cut me an' that . . . I'll let ya, cos ya my friend, I decided that now . . .

TWO. No . . .

ONE *grabs her by the hair.* TWO *screams.*

ONE. No. Come on.

TWO *manages to grab* ONE*'s arm and twists it behind her back.* ONE *screams and the two of them land heavily into the audience, giving enough time for audience members to scoot out of the way. This all happens pretty quickly.*

TWO. You fucking spastic!

ONE. No, May, no . . .

ONE *attempts to roll out of the hold, but* TWO *holds her in it, and speaks over the aggression.*

TWO. Ya like ya brother – no, don't cry, you fucking started it – you started first.

ONE. I ain't like my brother!

TWO *holds her in place.* ONE *is truly caught.*

TWO. Yeah. You are.

ONE. Then you're like your mam, ain't ya? If we're playing that.

Beat.

TWO. What?

TWO *drops* ONE*'s arm, and watches her stand up straight.* ONE *does a little dance.*

ONE (*checking T-shirt*). You ruined neck of this . . .

TWO. What?

ONE. I jus' wanna be friends.

TWO. WHAT?

ONE. How do you find the defendant Norma Joyce?

She clears a space and then jumps into it.

Not guilty.

How do you find the defendant Mary Norma?

Guilty.

MARY. What?

NORMA *goes around the audience, kissing everyone on the cheek. She then exits, leaving* MARY *alone.*

Nah . . . No. Not . . . it weren't just me . . .

MARY *sits in the corner as if she's waiting for something.*

What?

Then she realises she's in her cell and curls up. Then she straightens up, gets the cards out of her pocket and begins to shuffle them, gently humming 'Mrs Robinson'. Then she stops doing that, and curls up again. She finally looks up slowly at the walls around her.

ONE *doesn't come back for the bow.*

Part Two

SUPERSTAR

Characters

MARY

LUCY

STEVE

RAY

MARY *is sitting alone in a twin bed, scummy-looking B&B room. She looks fidgety. She is wearing the best clothes she can find – a miniskirt, which she keeps trying to make longer – and a fawn V-neck jumper and plastic 'leather' jacket. Her hair has been pushed up. It's 1978.*

She sits quietly for a moment, trying to get her fidgety hands under control, and then she brings out a mirror to redo her heavy mascara and lipstick.

Her friend LUCY *bursts in through the door, her arms cradling about fifteen bottles of cheap lager.* LUCY *is wearing similar clothes to* MARY *– but is much better at wearing them.*

LUCY. Quick! She's coming!

> MARY *runs over and helps her unload all the bottles into the bed. They pull back the covers and arrange the bottles under them.* MARY *then pulls off her jacket and jumps into bed on top of the bottles. It's not the most comfortable place to be.*
>
> *They wait pensively.*
>
> *After a moment* MARY *starts laughing and* LUCY *joins in.*

Ssh!

> LUCY *manages to control herself, and* MARY *copies. They wait.*
>
> *They wait some more.*

I'm sure she was following.

MARY. I've got a beer going right up my bum.

LUCY. Don't break them.

MARY. I'm gonna make you drink that one.

LUCY. I'm going to check.

MARY. Don't . . .

> LUCY *waits a moment longer, and then exits.* MARY
> *readjusts the bottles underneath her – and giggles to*
> *herself.* LUCY *comes running back in, with a giggle.*

LUCY. I heard her on the stairs.

> MARY *immediately lies flat, and pretends to sleep – she's*
> *pretty good at it – the bottles jiggle slightly underneath her –*
> *but then stop making any noise.* LUCY *looks around the*
> *room.*

What should I do?

MARY. Read a book.

LUCY. Then she'll know something's wrong.

> MARY *starts laughing.* LUCY *stops herself joining in.*

Stop it.

> MARY *stops laughing.*

> LUCY *sits down on the bed.*

 I'm going to pretend to pray.

> MARY *starts laughing again, but then stops herself, and*
> *resumes pretend sleep.*

> *The girls wait.*

I swear I heard her.

> MARY *sits up in bed.*

MARY. Is my make-up OK?

LUCY. She's not coming. She's not coming.

> STEVE *opens the wardrobe door and steps out.*

STEVE. Thank crap for that.

> RAY *rolls out from under the bed* MARY *isn't in. Both boys*
> *are wearing far too much hair gel.* RAY *is in a suit,* STEVE
> *isn't.* STEVE *has some element of his uniform on.*

RAY. They don't sweep under the beds here, you know that? Got dust in my earhole.

STEVE *looks at* MARY *irritably.*

STEVE. You need lifting out or what? I need a beer.

MARY. Oh. OK.

MARY *swings her legs over to the side of the bed and checks her skirt before standing up. The boys pull the top sheet off, and* STEVE *takes a beer and passes one to* RAY. STEVE *pulls out a pocket knife to open his beer with – he then throws the knife to* RAY, *who opens his too.*

STEVE. So –

LUCY. What?

STEVE. So what? That's right. So what?

LUCY. What?

STEVE. What you got us up here for?

LUCY. It was your idea.

STEVE. Was it arse. 'Come up to my room, Steve, me and my room-mate, we're gonna show you the real Blackpool sights.'

LUCY. I never did.

STEVE. Didn't she say something dirty about the Blackpool tower, Raymond?

RAY. Ray.

STEVE. You're not still going on about that?

RAY. That's what I'm called. Call me Ray. I feel all bunged up, you know? That dust under the bed.

STEVE. Concentrate, Ray. Didn't she say she'd show us the sights?

RAY. Yeah. She did.

STEVE. Or was it that other girl? Last night? Perhaps it was last night's girl. You think it was last night's girl, Ray?

RAY. The one with the lisp.

STEVE. Thass right. I'll sssshow you the Blackpool sssights.

RAY sits on MARY's bed. MARY is still standing up. She moves away from him. STEVE looks at LUCY with a trademark grin.

We're pulling your leg.

LUCY. I know you are.

STEVE. Laugh then.

LUCY. You gotta tell a joke first.

STEVE. Ooooh! Like a dagger to my heart.

LUCY. You want to see what I'd do to your cock.

STEVE. Is the right answer.

STEVE stands up and starts taking off his trousers.

LUCY. Hang on!

STEVE laughs again and redoes his trousers.

STEVE. You lot aren't good at these jokes, are you?

RAY. Steve –

STEVE. Sorry, I can't take him anywhere. He's a dirty one is Ray, taking his trousers down in public like that. Sorry, can't apologise enough. We're only on three days' leave. He can be a bit enthusiastic.

RAY. Steve –

LUCY. Nothing wrong with enthusiasm.

STEVE. No. You're right there.

Everyone sits quietly for a moment. RAY stands up and takes some cards out of his inside breast pocket.

RAY. Let's have a game of cards.

STEVE. Good idea. What do you girls play?

LUCY. We're not girls.

STEVE. You're not men dressed up, are you?

LUCY. We're women.

STEVE. What d'you women play?

LUCY. Dunno. What do you boys play?

STEVE. You name it, love – we'll play it.

LUCY. Give me some options.

STEVE. Whist. Nomination. Poker. Black Mariah. Pontoon.

LUCY. I can play Pontoon.

STEVE. We have a winner. Shall we use a bed as a table for our purposes?

MARY. I don't know Pontoon.

STEVE. Ray'll show you how to play. Why don't you go sit on his lap?

RAY. No, you go sit on Steve's lap, why don't you, love? His lap's nicer than mine.

STEVE. He just means I got a smaller cock. It isn't nicer.

RAY. It's nicer.

STEVE. It's not.

RAY. It's nicer.

STEVE. It's not.

MARY *smiles sadly, scratches her head, and goes and sits on the other side of the room.* LUCY *watches her.*

LUCY. One of you go sit with her. We come as a pair.

MARY. I'm OK.

LUCY. You sure?

MARY. Yeah, I just don't fancy cards, that's all.

LUCY. Well, we'll play over here, yeah?

RAY. Right. You know how to play?

LUCY. I said so, didn't I?

RAY *shuffles the cards extravagantly and begins to deal.*

RAY. Second card up?

STEVE. No. Keep it straight.

LUCY. Mary, I'll show you how to play.

MARY. I'm OK, ta.

STEVE. Well, mine's cod and chips if you're getting, love.

MARY. No, I'll stay here.

STEVE *laughs.* LUCY *checks her cards.*

STEVE. Can I have a fag in here?

LUCY. Well, she left ashtrays in.

STEVE. Ray?

RAY. Sure.

STEVE *passes* RAY *his packet, having taken out one for himself. They're cigarettes without filters (this is 1978). They both light up.*

LUCY. Gentlemen you are.

STEVE. Want one?

LUCY. Yeah.

LUCY *is given one and lights it. She checks her cards again.*

RAY. Twist?

LUCY. Yeah.

He deals her another card.

RAY. And again?

LUCY. Doesn't it carry on?

RAY. No.

LUCY. It's Steve's turn, isn't it?

RAY. No.

LUCY. OK, twist?

RAY. Right.

LUCY. It's 21, isn't it?

STEVE. You sure you've played this before?

RAY. Yeah, it's 21.

STEVE. Maybe me and Ray'll just have a game of cribbage and this one just sit it out and look pretty . . .

LUCY. Twist.

> RAY *deals her another card. She looks at it disappointed.*

I'm out I think. How much is a King?

STEVE. Ten.

LUCY. And the Queen is?

STEVE. Ten.

LUCY. That's ten points too? Does colour make a difference?

STEVE. No.

LUCY. They're the same colour. Queen and King.

> STEVE *takes* LUCY*'s cards off her and looks at them.*

STEVE. Yeah, you've got forty points.

LUCY. Don't just grab them!

STEVE. You're bust.

LUCY. You're not supposed to just grab them.

STEVE. You don't know how to play.

LUCY. I know I don't.

STEVE. So why did you say you did?

RAY. Shall we get out of here?

LUCY. Because I wanted to.

STEVE. Let's go down the amusements, shall we? Come on . . .
Even hop-a-long can come if she wants . . .

MARY. You talking about me?

LUCY. Can't.

STEVE. What?

LUCY. Doors lock at nine.

STEVE. You can kip at ours.

LUCY. Then she'll call the police. She said she took her
landlady job very seriously.

STEVE. Of all the places to choose. You chose here.

LUCY. First place we saw.

RAY. Tell her to sweep under the bed, then she can say what
time you're back in.

STEVE. Let her call the police. We fight for our country. Those
coppers'll let us anything for a polish of my buttonholes.

LUCY. Well, we don't want the police involved.

STEVE. Good girls, are we? Fair enough.

Pause.

LUCY. You can go if you want . . .

STEVE. We don't want to go.

RAY. Maybe we should go.

STEVE. If we stay, which of us you gonna kiss then?

LUCY. Isn't that a question!

STEVE. Been on my lips all night.

LUCY. Well, maybe me and Mary haven't decided yet.

STEVE. She's got her eye on Ray.

RAY. Like she has.

STEVE. What's wrong with her?

RAY. Nothing. You have her.

STEVE. She's a good-looking girl.

RAY. She's got funny eyes.

LUCY. She's got beautiful eyes, they're one of her best features.

RAY. She looks at me funny.

LUCY. You look at me funny.

RAY. I don't.

LUCY. You do.

MARY. I don't fancy them, Lucy.

LUCY. Neither?

MARY. Neither.

Pause. STEVE *laughs briefly, then shuts up*.

STEVE. Let's put the radio on, shall we?

MARY. I don't like the radio.

LUCY. You do.

STEVE. What do you like, Mary?

MARY. Questions . . .

STEVE. Like . . .

MARY (*suddenly forceful*). Like, you wanna be soldiers the rest of your life?

STEVE. No.

MARY. Do you, Ray?

RAY. No, I'm going to join my dad's plumbing business.

MARY. What soldiering you done?

STEVE. These are shit questions . . .

MARY. You don't like questions you should go, shouldn't they? Tell them, Lucy.

LUCY. Just tell her what soldiering you done.

STEVE. We just come back from Northern Ireland.

MARY. Holiday?

STEVE. No.

RAY. Can we put the radio on now?

LUCY. Have another beer?

STEVE. It's not some great secret, just none of your business.

RAY. We haven't seen anything bad or anything. It's not like that . . .

LUCY. It's OK. We didn't think that.

Pause. Everyone's a bit pissed off now.

STEVE. Why you friends with her? You don't seem to have much between you.

LUCY. Why are you friends with him? He keeps trying to cop off with the girl you fancy.

STEVE. Yeah, but he's a laugh.

LUCY. So's Mary.

STEVE. Well, it ain't my kind of humour.

LUCY. She isn't like this all the time, you've dented her confidence.

MARY. No, they haven't.

LUCY. She's a beautiful girl.

MARY. No, I'm not.

LUCY. Yes you are.

Pause.

We should talk about something else now. Mary's asked her question now.

RAY. I wasn't saying . . . you've just got funny eyes . . .

STEVE. They're fine.

MARY. It's OK.

STEVE. I'm fed up of talking.

LUCY. Well, the mood's not right for anything else.

STEVE. Yeah. It is.

> STEVE *stands up and turns on the radio: 'If You Can't Give Me Love' by Suzi Quatro. The song is halfway through the first verse. Everyone immediately brightens. This is a cracking tune.*

MARY. I like this one.

RAY. Cracking, isn't it?

MARY. I like her voice.

> STEVE *takes* LUCY*'s hand –* LUCY *lets him – and they start to dance, country style.*

STEVE. See, that's the noise I hope angels make. Sound like hers. Be boring if they were all (*Like a choirboy.*) 'Ahhhhhh.'

> MARY *giggles as* LUCY *is spun towards her.* LUCY *almost falls, but* RAY *catches her, and she laughs and then goes back to* STEVE.

> *Everyone joins in with the chorus of the song.*

> RAY *mouths along with the verse, he knows all the words, performing it to* MARY, *who thinks this is hilarious. Suzi Quatro's voice coming out of* RAY*'s mouth.*

> STEVE *kisses* LUCY, *distracting* RAY *from his lyrics.* MARY *and* RAY *watch in silence as* LUCY *and* STEVE *continue to kiss throughout the song.*

> *The chorus comes on again,* MARY *sings along, but* RAY *doesn't sing this time, and* LUCY *and* STEVE *have their mouths full.* MARY *stops singing.*

> LUCY *and* STEVE *break off.*

STEVE. You taste like marmalade.

LUCY *giggles*. RAY *turns off the radio*.

(*To* RAY.) Don't be stupid.

RAY. Me and Mary were trying to talk. Couldn't hear ourselves think.

MARY. That's true.

STEVE *sits down. He tries to get* LUCY *to sit on his lap. She doesn't*.

STEVE. So what were we talking about?

RAY. What Mary does for a living . . .

MARY. No, we weren't.

RAY. Go on . . .

MARY. No . . .

RAY. Go on.

MARY. I work in a chemist.

RAY. You work there too, Lucy?

LUCY. I don't know. Do I?

MARY. No.

LUCY. Don't I?

MARY. No.

LUCY *giggles*.

LUCY. No, that's right, I work in a florist down the road.

STEVE. What's going on?

LUCY. You want some flowers? Can get you a good deal . . .

RAY. What?

STEVE. What are you two like?

MARY. You wouldn't tell us what you do.

STEVE. Yeah, we would.

MARY. No, you wouldn't.

LUCY. We've run away.

STEVE. From where?

LUCY. From . . . an orphanage.

STEVE. Fuck! How old are you?

LUCY (*giggling*). No, not really, we've run from prison.

RAY. What?

LUCY. Nothing serious. Open plan. GBH, me; murder, her.

RAY. What?

MARY. Self-defence though.

LUCY. Go on then. What's the worst thing you've seen in
    Northern Ireland?

RAY. We haven't. We haven't been there long. It's been fine.

LUCY. Right. Well then, this is a bit of fun, isn't it? Shall we
    have the radio back on? Or another go at that card game –
    I'm sure I could do better.

STEVE. GBH?

LUCY. Another girl, don't worry. I wouldn't hurt you.

STEVE. No, I wasn't . . . I wasn't saying it like that . . .

    Pause. LUCY *considers the room*.

LUCY. Well, this is a bit of fun.

RAY. Yeah.

    Pause. LUCY *opens a beer, and passes one to* MARY, *who
    opens hers*.

STEVE. You've escaped?

LUCY. Listen to him! You sounded like a robot. Just for the
    weekend, we'll go back.

MARY. You can take us if you like. Saves hitching, and you
    could get your picture in the paper.

STEVE. How did it – how did it happen?

LUCY. The escape?

STEVE. GBH.

LUCY. Oh, she was shagging with my brother. I just pushed her off the top of these steps we have by my local. She broke both her legs.

STEVE. Right.

LUCY. Do you want some mouthwash? So you can gargle the taste of me out of your mouth?

STEVE. No.

LUCY. You can if you want. I won't be offended.

STEVE. No.

LUCY. OK. You really seen nothing – all the time you've been in the army?

RAY. A guy got his hand blown off during a drill once.

LUCY. That sounds good.

RAY. Well, not blown off, but damaged.

LUCY. OK.

    Pause.

RAY. You hear stories about the other stuff – but we haven't seen it –

STEVE. We'd like to.

RAY. Well, not the bad stuff . . .

STEVE. No.

RAY. Shall I put the radio back on?

MARY. No.

    Pause.

STEVE. We took these girls out last night – they were in a room like this one – had to shunt 'em over the wall. Walked all the way down the pier and back with them, didn't we?

RAY. Shut up, Steve.

STEVE. What? They put out, didn't they? I was just saying we – I was just pointing out – we're all here for the same thing, aren't we?

RAY. Don't be daft.

STEVE. I got to choose last night's victims, Ray here chose you two. He liked the way you were sitting together with your candyfloss on the beach in the rain.

RAY. Steve . . .

STEVE. What's wrong with telling them about other girls? You liked it when I told the lisp story.

RAY. That wasn't true. You're making us sound cheap now.

LUCY. He's making us sound cheap more like.

STEVE. I'm just being honest.

MARY. I like it. We're just like all the others . . .

RAY. He didn't mean that.

MARY. No, I like it, it's normal, isn't it? I like normal.

LUCY. Well, I don't like it that much. I, for one, am a bit special.

STEVE *laughs*.

STEVE. Here's my question. Either of you got a boyfriend? Waiting for you when you get out?

LUCY. Mary doesn't.

MARY. No.

LUCY. I do. He's called Matthew.

STEVE. He must've been upset – you doing what you did . . .

LUCY. Not really. Upset when the judge gave me nine months. Tried to get me pregnant before I went in – said if he was going to do without it for nine months he'd rather it'd be for a reason . . .

STEVE. You can still shag if a girl's pregnant.

LUCY. Had a lot of them, have you?

STEVE. Two or three.

STEVE *laughs. No one else does.*

Why didn't you go to him then? Seeing as you're out?

LUCY. He'd drive me straight back, that's why.

MARY. And you wanted normal.

LUCY. Shut up about normal!

RAY. I've got a girl waiting for me. She thinks we're getting married. She was well miffed off when I joined up. Said I was running away from a commitment.

MARY. What's she called?

RAY. I'd rather not say.

MARY. Case I go find her and kill her? I'm a jealous slag, me.

RAY *laughs, and then laughs again.* MARY *joins in.*

LUCY. Told you she was funny.

RAY. Alice. She works in a florist actually.

LUCY. She doesn't!

RAY. Yeah.

LUCY. She's nice . . .

RAY. Yeah. She's not that pretty . . .

STEVE. But she's got a lovely set of legs on her. He fell in love with her in summer, didn't know she'd have to wear tights in the winter.

RAY. No . . .

LUCY. She sounds nice.

RAY. She's not, but I'm committed.

LUCY. That's why you're here, is it?

STEVE *laughs.*

STEVE. Yeah, you gotta give her that one.

RAY. She has got nice legs.

LUCY. You want another beer?

RAY. Yeah.

MARY. Mine was younger than me – little boy, he pulled a knife, so I stabbed him with it. They would have believed me, but it happened twice.

RAY. Right.

MARY. They don't believe you can be unlucky enough to use self-defence twice. Just so you know.

LUCY. But she did.

MARY. Yeah. Just so you know.

Pause.

LUCY. Anyone got any food?

STEVE. Have we, Ray?

RAY. We've got some biscuits I think.

LUCY. Oh, I love biscuits.

STEVE. Go find the biscuits, Ray.

MARY *turns on the radio. There's a blast of disc jockey.* RAY *has found the biscuits in his satchel, and passes them to* LUCY *who starts to open them.*

LUCY. Turn it off, May.

MARY *turns the radio off. She then, quite bravely, goes over and sits by* RAY. LUCY *eats biscuits with her mouth open.*

MARY. I just thought we could dance.

LUCY. Told you that you liked it. Mary's always dancing. When we're on work we're allowed to have music on, she always dances. The guards don't mind, they're used to her.

MARY. You can put your arm around me if you want.

RAY. OK.

LUCY (*halfway through her third biscuit already*). Does that mean I've got this one, May?

MARY. Long as this one's happy?

RAY *thinks a moment*, MARY *laughs*.

RAY. I'm happy.

MARY. I think he thinks I'm a celebrity now.

RAY. I'm happy with my arm around you.

LUCY. Which means Steve's got me, as long as he's OK with it?

MARY. He better be. He's lucky.

STEVE. I know I am.

The foursome sit in pairs.

MARY. So was it horrible? When it happened to his hand?

RAY. Worried me a bit. Plumber's nothing without his hands.

MARY. Can't imagine a one-handed soldier's much cock.

RAY (*laughs*). True. What's he doing now, Steve?

STEVE. I think he works in stores.

MARY. What's it like on the streets then? Walking round with your gun?

STEVE. We're on the border.

RAY. We really haven't seen much yet. When we go back there's a chance of Belfast, which would be good.

STEVE. We're all quite hopeful for that.

MARY. Maybe we'll escape to Belfast next time, what do you think, Lucy?

LUCY. No, I'm out in two, aren't I?

MARY. Are you?

LUCY. Yeah.

RAY. You won't get more on for running away?

LUCY. No. They're quite good about it. Maybe a month more. Couple of weeks. Nothing more than that.

MARY. Yeah.

LUCY. Mary's seen us all come and go, haven't you?

MARY. I suppose I have.

LUCY. She's in longer than the rest of us.

MARY. Why they let me dance I suppose. I've never thought of it like that. I thought it was just because they liked me.

LUCY. They do like you.

MARY. I catch them looking at me sometimes though. Everyone does. Trying to work out what kind of animal I am.

LUCY. I don't.

MARY. I'd like to be a dolphin I think. Not because they're helpful or nice or like Flipper.

LUCY. We watch that all the time.

RAY. We watch that in mess.

MARY. Just because they don't even tell you when they're doing something nice – I hate people who tell you when they're doing something nice. You tell me sometimes, Lucy, and I don't like it.

LUCY. OK.

MARY. Sorry.

LUCY. No, that's OK. You told me now.

MARY. I don't need them to tell me I'm pretty, I think I am, and it's worse if you tell them they have to.

LUCY. OK, you told me.

MARY. Well . . .

Pause. LUCY *walks floutily over to the beer stash and takes herself another beer.*

RAY. I'm the same. It's why I don't like him calling me Raymond.

STEVE. That's your name.

RAY. Makes me sound slow.

STEVE. You're not slow.

RAY. I was slow at school.

MARY. I was the cleverest in mine.

Pause.

RAY. You are pretty, you're really pretty.

MARY. Just got funny eyes, I know.

RAY. No, they've settled down now. They're beautiful eyes now. You got eyes like Lana Turner really. You're beautiful.

MARY. Well, my legs aren't up to much.

RAY. If I wanted legs I'd have gone home for my leave.

MARY. Yeah. You would've done, wouldn't you?

RAY. Yeah.

MARY. So there was a girl . . . with special green eyes. The eyes were so special she had to keep them in a box because her dad said that they were better than she was, that they were her best feature, and so much her best feature that they had to be kept, to be protected.

STEVE. You telling us a story?

LUCY. She's just being weird.

MARY. Every night she would take them out and she would put them in her eyes, to see again how beautiful they were. But because she didn't have eyes in the rest of the day – because she was walking around with dusty eye-sockets – that just accumulated dirt because they were on front of her face and your face gets more dirt than anything else.

Because of that, she was getting the eyes worse and worse, she couldn't clean her eye-sockets out, she knew she was getting worse and worse, and she realised she couldn't wear the eyes ever again otherwise they'd be ruined forever. So every day she would get up and she would wash her hands with bleach and she would just touch the eyes. That was her special treat. And then one day, her birthday, she realised she couldn't go on without trying on the eyes again, and so she poured bleach in her eye sockets and she fitted the eyes in. The eyes allowed her to watch her face dissolve from the bleach.

Pause.

RAY. Did you just imagine that on the spot? Make that up?

MARY. Yeah. I did.

RAY. That's good, that. That's a good story, wasn't it, Steve?

STEVE. Bit odd for my taste, Ray, and not enough jokes.

MARY. Sorry. Shouldn't have said all that. Sometimes I feel too happy, do you know what I mean? I feel too happy.

RAY. I know what you mean. Sometimes I feel too happy too.

MARY. Jittery or something . . .

RAY. Yeah. I know what you mean.

MARY. Flibbertigibbet.

STEVE. She like this in jail?

LUCY. Yeah. Some of the time.

MARY. I'm either quiet or flibbertigibbet, aren't I?

LUCY. Everyone loves her.

MARY. No. They don't.

LUCY. It was my idea – to escape, because there was a time after wash where I saw we could get out – I could have chosen anyone to go with me and I chose Mary, didn't I, Mary?

MARY. Yeah. You did.

STEVE. That's funny cos it was my idea to come to Blackpool, wasn't it, Ray?

RAY. Loads of squaddies go to Blackpool. There's a boat.

STEVE. Yeah, but my idea to come this weekend, wasn't it? I could have taken anyone and I took Ray.

RAY. I had to lend you for your fare.

STEVE *laughs*.

STEVE. Yeah. That's right.

MARY *stands up and turns on the radio: 'It's a Heartache' by Bonnie Tyler. It comes in halfway through the song.*

She takes RAY*'s hand, he lets her dance with him. She's quite a good dancer.* LUCY *laughs as she does a twirl. Then* MARY *stops, after barely thirty seconds of it. She turns off the radio.*

MARY. No, I don't want the attention.

RAY. What?

MARY. Let's be normal here, like the other girls, not dancing and having everyone looking at me.

RAY. No one was looking.

LUCY. We won't look any more, May, if you don't want us to.

MARY. No, I'd prefer to do different. Normal.

LUCY. Shall we kiss them, May? Is that normal?

STEVE. Look at you!

MARY. Yeah. That's normal. Long as no one looks.

LUCY. I won't look. I'll be kissing him.

STEVE. You gotta ask first, love . . .

LUCY *kisses* STEVE *passionately.*

LUCY. Like I do. You'd take anything, you.

STEVE. True.

LUCY *kisses him again.* MARY *hesitates. She sits on the bed.* RAY *sits beside her.*

RAY. You don't have to if you don't want to . . .

MARY. No, it's OK . . .

LUCY *pushes* STEVE *back on the bed, and starts taking her clothes off.*

STEVE. Like that, is it?

LUCY. You calling me a fast lady?

STEVE. Depends if you want me to take my trousers off or not . . .

LUCY. You OK, May?

MARY. Yeah, I'm fine.

RAY. We'll just sit like this a minute.

LUCY *pulls off her top.* MARY *starts fidgeting her hands on her lap.*

MARY. Were you with him? When his hand got taken?

RAY. No. Well, I was on the same exercise, but I didn't see it. We just all crowded round to look at the blood.

MARY. Did you like it?

RAY. No.

MARY. Good. I'm pleased. I don't like people who like blood.

LUCY. Mary, OK?

MARY. You just do what you're doing, OK?

LUCY. If you want me to stop . . .

STEVE. You stop now, my balls'll go blue permanent.

LUCY. Shut up. Mary?

MARY. It's fine.

LUCY. OK.

RAY *and* MARY *listen as* STEVE *and* LUCY *get further entangled.*

RAY. I don't really want to go to Belfast. I'm quite scared of all that, not bad scared just . . . you know. I only signed up to get away from Alice.

MARY. I don't want to go back to jail.

RAY. Shall we escape somewhere then?

MARY. No.

RAY. OK.

MARY. You're going to be a really good plumber though.

RAY. I know.

LUCY *and* STEVE *are starting to have sex.*

MARY. Can I tell you a secret, Ray? I'm twenty-one today. Haven't told anyone.

RAY. Twenty-one, are you? That's good.

MARY. And this is the first time I've been out of prison since I was eleven.

RAY. You went in when you were eleven? That's young.

MARY. They're going to let me out in nine months or so, did you know that?

RAY. No.

MARY. Mary Bell back on the streets.

RAY. Bell, is it? Your surname.

MARY. You don't know who I am?

RAY. Well, I do now, Mary Bell. It's a nice name. I'll think of it when I think of you.

MARY. You are slow, aren't you? Most people would know who I was.

RAY. You're a celebrity then?

MARY. Sort of. Yeah. I am.

Pause.

RAY. Mary Bell, is it?

MARY. Do you mind? Who I am?

RAY. Well, maybe I would but I don't really know who you are.

MARY. That's good.

RAY. Besides, I like you, don't I?

MARY. That's good too.

Pause.

I think my life's going to be shit.

RAY. No, it won't.

MARY. It will be.

RAY. Don't think like that.

MARY *is thinking like that.* RAY *tries to help her out of her hole.*

Go on then. What job you going to get when you get out?

MARY. Do you like newspapers?

RAY. Me? Yeah.

MARY. I always wondered – what if you took one paper from one day and just decided to investigate every story in it. Just decided that was all you were going to do with your life. Politics, murders – you investigate them all – what was said, who said it, the journalists who wrote it. I like how quick the stories are in newspapers – but imagine if you could just make them long.

RAY. Yeah.

MARY. That's what job I'd do.

RAY. Is that a job?

STEVE. OI!

LUCY. What?

STEVE. Don't twist 'em.

LUCY. You want this or not?

STEVE. Oh, that's nice . . .

Pause. LUCY *and* STEVE *continue rutting in the background.* RAY *turns to* MARY *with an expectant smile on his face, he leans in to kiss her.*

MARY. I haven't done this before.

RAY. Oh. Which bit?

MARY. All of it. Kissing. All of it.

RAY. Oh.

MARY. But I'd like to try.

RAY. Right.

MARY. If you . . . still want to.

RAY. Yeah, I do.

MARY. Good.

Pause.

So . . . you gotta tell me how to do it . . .

RAY. Right. Well. Lift your head up. Tilt it towards me. That's smashing.

He kisses her. Then breaks off, laughing.

Your lips feel like bullets. Soften them.

MARY. How?

RAY. Just imagine you're . . . I don't know. Soften them.

MARY. I'll lick them.

RAY. No . . . just concentrate on them being soft.

MARY. OK.

He kisses her again.

RAY. There we go. Perfect. What d'you think of that?

MARY. Yeah. Quite nice.

RAY. Try again?

MARY. Do I feel like normal? Like the girls you're normally with?

RAY *laughs*.

RAY. Yeah, you do. Try again?

MARY. Yeah.

Lights down.

A Nick Hern Book

Stacy and *Fanny and Faggot* first published in Great Britain as a paperback original in 2007 by Nick Hern Books Limited, 14 Larden Road, London W3 7ST

Reprinted 2009, 2012

Stacy and *Fanny and Faggot* copyright © 2007 Jack Thorne

Jack Thorne has asserted his right to be identified as the author of this work

Cover image: 5065 Lift
Cover design: Ned Hoste, 2H

Typeset by Nick Hern Books
Printed in the UK by Mimeo Ltd, Huntingdon, Cambridgeshire PE29 6XX

A CIP catalogue record for this book is available from the British Library

ISBN   978 1 85459 989 6